D1109581

SLAVE STEALERS

SLAVE STEALERS

TRUE ACCOUNTS OF
SLAVE RESCUES
THEN and NOW

TIMOTHY BALLARD

SHADOW
MOUNTAIN

© 2018 Rockwell Group Inc.

Visit us at shadowmountain.com

Library of Congress Cataloging-in-Publication Data
(CIP on file)
ISBN 978-1-62972-484-3

Printed in the United States of America
Publishers Printing, Salt Lake City, UT

10 9 8 7 6 5 4 3 2 1

To my best friend, Katherine,
and to our children

*"Reader, be assured this narrative is no fiction.
I am aware that some of my adventures may seem incredible;
but they are, nevertheless, strictly true."*

—*Harriet Jacobs, 1861*
Preface to her book, Incidents in the Life of a Slave Girl

CONTENTS

Tim Ballard and Mike Tomlin

FOREWORD

MIKE TOMLIN
Pittsburgh Steelers Head Coach

I was raised in urban Virginia in a black community. I didn't
particularly trust white people. So when I was told one day
by my high school administrators to get in a police car driven
by a white cop, you can imagine what expletives went running
through my mind.

The car ride wasn't what you might be thinking. (Thank
goodness!) I had actually been selected to attend a leadership
program outside of Philadelphia at the Freedoms Foundation at
Valley Forge. (I would later learn, incidentally, that Tim Ballard,
the author of this book, had attended this same program as a
youth. In light of how our paths would cross later, perhaps this
was more providential than coincidental.) The cop, Officer Steve
Rutherford, had for some reason volunteered to drive me and
another classmate who had been selected up to Valley Forge to
attend the program. Being one of two black kids sitting in the
back of a police car driven through two states by a white cop was,
though totally innocent and benign, extremely uncomfortable,
to say the least. As you might guess, the car ride up could pretty
much be described as "dead silent." Beyond the occasional awkward glance I threw toward the officer—wondering who he *really*
was and what he was *really* planning on doing with me—I dared
not hazard any other form of communication with him.

But then something happened. He spoke. And he spoke kind

words. I replied politely. A simple conversation ensued. I can't even remember what we said, but I remember what I felt, because it was the last thing I expected to feel. *Friendship.*

After the conference ended, Officer Rutherford was waiting in the parking lot to drive us home. The ride home was much different. We talked the whole way. We joked, we laughed. All of a sudden, our relationship had nothing at all to do with how either of us looked or what professions we had chosen. We were just two human beings, both in the same image of God, interested in the same things, laughing at the same jokes, dealing with some of the same life problems, and just being friends.

As my high school years passed, I stayed in touch with Officer Rutherford. I grew to like him more and more. I eventually graduated and left home to attend the College of William and Mary, where I had been blessed to win a football scholarship. Moving to a different city and playing football on a team made up of young men from around the country of every color and creed opened my eyes and softened my heart in important ways. I began to realize that there were actually a lot of people like Officer Rutherford. I didn't have to automatically distrust and hate people anymore based on a false prejudice.

One day at college, I received a phone call from home. It was one of the worst phone calls of my entire life.

"Officer Rutherford is dead." Those are the only words I remember from that call.

I dropped the phone. I couldn't believe it. I couldn't process it. My heart hurt in ways I didn't think possible, especially after I heard what had happened. As it turned out, Officer Rutherford had volunteered to participate in a police investigation of the strangest kind. A few thugs from my hometown had been ordering pizzas delivered to certain locales, then robbing the pizza man clean when he showed up. Officer Rutherford agreed to go undercover as "pizza delivery boy" one night, and, as fate would have it, he ended up delivering pizza to the thieves. When they made their move, he dropped to the ground as if submitting to their demands. But one of them noticed that he was carrying a gun, panicked, and shot him, killing him almost instantly.

Officer Rutherford was a good man. He had a job. It was a tough job, but he did it to serve others. And he lost his life over it, leaving behind a grieving wife. My broken heart broke even harder when I learned that the thugs in this case who took his life over pizza money were a couple of old high school classmates of mine.

After this incident, I was determined to be better, to look deeper, and to search for the truth in humanity and society that too often gets hidden by prejudice. Finding that truth can be very difficult. There are deep-seated issues driven by race—some real, some perceived—that stand as stumbling blocks to a more peaceful America. But it's a peaceful America that I *want* to see someday, one that I believe we *can* see someday. Like I said, though, it's tough to find it through the hate and divisiveness that plague our society. It's tough to find even for people like me, who are desperately searching for it; it's impossible to find for people who refuse to even try.

As an NFL coach, I get a front-and-center view of this sort of disunity. Certainly the world has seen how the NFL sometimes serves as a sort of microcosm of the nation as a whole. And I don't think I've ever seen the NFL as pained and plagued by divisiveness as it is right now.

For years I have been praying and pondering for a solution to this ever-growing problem. Then, not long ago, I stumbled on one: a highly unexpected one. It's a solution connected to the book you are about to read. It's connected to the deep friendship that my fellow Pittsburgh Steelers and I have forged with Tim Ballard and the brave men and women at Operation Underground Railroad (O.U.R.)—a nonprofit organization made up of former Navy SEALs, CIA operators, and Homeland Security agents who dedicate their lives to infiltrating the black markets of child sex slavery in order to liberate these innocent captives and lock up their predators. After serving in the CIA, then later as a special agent and undercover operator for the Department of Homeland Security, where he worked mostly on cases involving sex crimes against children, Tim founded O.U.R. as a means to attack this vicious plague from a different angle.

But before I can fully explain how O.U.R. helped me find the unique solution I was pondering in connection to the national hate and disunity we are all witnessing, I need to first tell you about the circumstances under which I *met* Tim and O.U.R.— for it was my process of discovering them that helped me see the light I was looking for.

It began with a chance encounter with former Navy SEAL Dave Lopez, who owned a tactical training company. I had tracked Dave down with the thought of hiring him to provide some tactical security training for certain players on my team. Dave would later tell me that, while he had come to Pittsburgh that day excited about the prospect of negotiating a business deal, as he walked into my office, something told him to stop. He just *knew.* He wasn't to even bring up the training opportunity. Instead, he was to introduce me to an organization that he worked for—an organization called Operation Underground Railroad.

I was instantly fascinated. I began asking Dave about his past and how he got involved with the organization. As I listened to his story, it sounded all too familiar.

Like me, he was born and raised in Virginia. And like me, he was raised under the dark, cold banner of prejudice. But *his* prejudice had come from the other side of the coin from where mine had come from. He was from white, rural Virginia. Due to a few contentious moments that he had experienced in his youth with a handful of black kids—moments he now admits he had misread for the worst—Dave decided that a little racism was justified. He viewed all things through this newfound prism of race, including a tainted view of history. He proudly waved his Confederate flag, became a Lincoln hater, and sided against any racial minority claims.

"I was a stupid, lost kid back then," he told me regretfully. "I was full of hate and spread lies about the past, present, and future."

But, like me, he had a conversion. He moved out of his hometown and did volunteer work in Central America. He then joined the navy and was deployed as a SEAL to Iraq, Africa, and Eastern Europe. Everything changed. Like me, he saw that *all* people really are made in the image of God. He learned we are all brothers and sisters, equal in heaven's eyes. And he learned, in ways too difficult to even mention, that black and white both bleed the same red.

"Then," Dave continued, "I found Operation Underground Railroad—the capstone of my long journey of self-discovery, from dark to light, from hate to love."

He paused and looked at me intently. He seemed to be digging in deep to describe to me what he wanted to say next. I waited patiently.

"Children," he said quietly, his deep emotions causing his voice to crack just a bit. "There is nothing like pulling a child out of the deep hell of slavery to convince you more powerfully of what's *really* important in life. There is nothing like witnessing that kind of abuse, and being part of a solution to that abuse, that more readily softens your heart and soul and gets you quicker to a place beyond racial and other societal divides. It's like going from dark to light in a nanosecond."

As Dave left my office, my heart was so full. There are no words in the English language to describe what I felt. First and foremost, I was having a hard time processing the reality and magnitude of child slavery in the world today. I was anxious (nervous, but anxious) to review the video links Dave had provided me, which showed actual footage from child rescue operations that O.U.R. had conducted around the world. When I got home, my wife and I watched the footage, along with a documentary about O.U.R., and we emptied an entire tissue box in the process.

The next day I continued to ponder the whole situation. I thought of the innocent child victims I had seen on the television screen the night before. I thought of a Haitian father named Guesno Mardy I had learned about in the documentary. Guesno's child was kidnapped and trafficked, and O.U.R. is on the case. (You will learn the details of this story of tragedy and hope in this book.) I thought of what Dave had told me about his past, I thought about my own past, and I thought of the peace and light I had been searching for my entire adult life—something that could hopefully heal the land I love from this sickness of hate that plagues it more and more each day.

Then a thought struck me that I felt I needed to share with Tim Ballard. So I called him and invited him and his team to Steelers summer training camp. And they came. I invited them to spend the week in the team dormitories. I wanted to see full integration between O.U.R. and the Pittsburgh Steelers. I gave Tim the opportunity to brief the entire team on the O.U.R. mission. I saw tears form in the eyes of some of the toughest men in the NFL. The thought and solution I had had was proving correct. I now needed to share it with Tim. I asked him to meet me for dinner after practice.

"I have a secret," I told Tim as we sat down to eat. "I almost feel a little dirty about it." Tim just smiled, anxious to hear me out.

"The reason I feel dirty," I continued, "is that what I'm going to say may make you think I have an ulterior motive for inviting you here. And I kind of do." Tim and I both chuckled.

"There is nothing more important on this planet than rescuing abused children," I said, "and I want that clear. But I've been thinking. There may be another powerful benefit to this cause beyond that important goal. There may be a healing power in this mission—a healing power that our nation needs now."

Tim nodded, seeming to know where I was going next.

"Let me ask you, Tim," I continued, "why do you call your foundation Operation Underground Railroad?"

Tim's face lit up. "That name did not come to me casually," he said. I instantly saw his passion swell as he prepared to tell a story from history.

"The original Underground Railroad is what inspired me to retire from the government and start a rescue foundation. After hunting traffickers and liberating children around the world for over a decade, I realized something. We can't do this alone. The problem is too big and growing too fast. We need everyone. We need every nationality, race, religion—every color and creed—if we are to solve this problem. And that's the pattern of the original Underground! Think about it! In a time when hate, prejudice, and racism ruled the country, this nineteenth-century band of organizers put their collective foot down. Black people embraced white people, white people embraced black people, they both embraced all other types of people. Then they dropped their prejudices and differences, linked arms, and walked into the darkness together because they found a problem bigger than any one of them. They hated human suffering. They hated captivity of the human mind and body. So they marched in together to stop it. To stop slavery. And *that's* what we need today!"

Tim was speaking my language. He was articulating the very thoughts I had been having. We found ourselves on the exact same wavelength. Can you imagine what would happen to this nation if we could get everyone focused on the cause of rescuing children? Not only would our principal goal of rescuing kids be more readily met, but something else might just happen in the process. Healing! Personal healing. Community healing. National healing. No, our problems surrounding race, social injustice, and misunderstanding would not instantly go away. But instead of perpetuating a seemingly endless argument that only drives us further apart and further from peace, at least we would all now be in the same room. We would all be focused on a problem we can *all* agree is a problem—a problem worth the effort of locking arms and joining hands around.

Then, as we fight the good fight together, as we crawl into the trenches together, we might get to know each other, just like I got to know Officer Rutherford, just like Dave Lopez got to know his fellow soldiers in the field. Then we can talk. Then we can find understanding. Then we can find solutions to our many other societal problems. Instead of fighting each other, we will be serving each other and serving alongside each other. Instead of dividing, we will be uniting. Instead of hate, love. Instead of dark, light.

"It's time to resurrect the Underground Railroad!" I declared to Tim with a smile on my face and my fist extended to him.

"Let's do it!" he responded, a knowing look in his eye as he bumped my fist with his.

So, how do we do it? How does this formula work? What does a modern-day Underground Railroad look like? How do we take the lessons from the original foundation and apply them to the new? How does the Underground Railroad rescue kids today? How does it rescue our hearts and souls? In this book, Tim Ballard will guide you through exciting, dangerous, and emotional rescue stories from the Underground Railroad, both from the old one and the new, and in the process he will answer these very questions.

After my conversation with Tim, I didn't want to wait for the publication of this book before I started digging in. I began to study the Underground. I became reacquainted with heroes like Harriet Tubman, Frederick Douglass, and other brave leaders of that awesome movement. But there was one operator in that historical movement that I had never heard of before, and his story was more than intriguing to me.

His name was Jonathan Walker, and he was a white nineteenth-century sea captain from Massachusetts. He took a job in the South and saw slavery. And he hated it. So he did what he could. On one occasion in 1844, he made the risky decision to help several American slaves escape from the Deep South and into the Caribbean. He attempted to smuggle them out on his ship, but he was caught on the high seas. He was arrested and dragged into a United States courtroom. Thereafter, he was prosecuted, jailed, fined, tied to a pillory, and, as part of his sentence, branded. Yes, branded like cattle. The blazing iron brand contained two letters: *SS,* for "Slave Stealer." Those letters were seared into the palm of his hand so all might know his crime and mock him in his shame.

Well, the punishment backfired. When the abolitionists in the North learned of what had happened, they got together and bailed him out, paid his fine, and helped get him back to the North. Captain Walker didn't cower at all. He joined up with his brothers and sisters of all colors and creeds and dedicated his life to eradicating slavery. And he did it all with his palm open. Yes, he wore his punishment as a badge of honor. He showed the world his branded hand so all would know who he was. He was proud to be a Slave Stealer.

I later learned that Tim and his operators host a podcast in order to tell these amazing stories of rescue and restoration from both the old and the new Underground. To honor Jonathan Walker and all those who risked life and limb to liberate the captive, they named their program *Slave Stealer Podcast.* As my team was becoming converted to O.U.R.'s mission, I found it amusing that there is only one team in the NFL that kind of shares the same nickname as these brave operators—and it is us! The Pittsburgh *Steelers.*

Then it all became more than just amusing when I realized something else. The only team in the NFL that shares the precise black-and-gold color scheme of O.U.R. is, again, the Pittsburgh Steelers. Tim chose those colors for O.U.R. years before we ever knew each other and before Tim was a fan of our team. Coincidence? Maybe. Or maybe there really are tokens from heaven given to confirm our callings in life. Maybe we should all do better at seeking those messages and callings. As you read this book, you will see that's exactly what our heroes of the past have always done. And as you read this book, that's exactly what I'm asking *you* to do.

My name is Mike Tomlin. I'm a Pittsburgh Steeler. And I'm a Slave Stealer!

PART 1
THE STORIES

INTRODUCTION

For well over a decade I've traveled the world working as an undercover operator in an attempt to infiltrate and dismantle networks within the dark world of child trafficking. I began doing this work as a U.S. special agent, then later carried out the mission as a private operator for governments all around the world through my foundation, Operation Underground Railroad (O.U.R.). I've received extensive government training to do this type of work. But I also received training from another place—a place that may seem strange to many, but to me, it has become a base camp for knowledge and inspiration in my fight against the kidnapping, trafficking, and exploitation of children. That place is *history*—specifically, the history born of the abolitionist movements of the nineteenth century.

My instructors in this unique "training program" have been my heroes of this historical movement: heroes like Harriet Tubman, Frederick Douglass, Harriet Beecher Stowe, William Still, Levi Coffin, and many others. But of all these heroes of the nineteenth century, there is one who, more than anyone else, has instructed me, inspired me, taught me, and guided me in my efforts to fight modern-day slavery. Her name was Harriet Jacobs, and she was born a slave in 1813 in the small North Carolina town of Edenton. But she wouldn't remain a slave. The story of her struggle and her triumph in fighting for her freedom so that she might help others out of slavery has provided more insight and instruction for me and O.U.R. than perhaps any other human source. The purpose of this book is to explain *why* and *how*, and to encourage you, the reader, to be similarly enlightened by her story.

But before getting into that story, and before explaining what it is exactly about Harriet Jacobs that stands out to me, I want to first explain what led me to Jacobs and her colleagues in the first place. That process was personal to me. This is important to understand up front because it can be problematic to make nonpersonal, general comparisons between historical slavery, often called the transatlantic slave trade, and modern-day slavery. Though both forms of abuse should certainly be called *slavery* (as there is no other word for what happened then and what is happening now), it's important to distinguish between the two evils. For there are marked differences between the two. We must be careful to preserve the integrity of the stories of both the old and new slavery and to protect each story and those players in it. Too often, we assume the two forms are identical, which can cause us to misuse terms and labels, make faulty applications, and cannibalize history.

That said, we are also doing ourselves, and those victims who need us most, a great disservice if we fail to learn what we can from the past. There *are* parallels. There are lessons to be learned! These lessons and parallels are more safely made in case-specific applications rather than in general, simplistic, and broad-sweeping conclusions. But the urgency of the cause calls on us to learn everything we can so that we might help those who suffer the most.

Slavery today is a big business. To illustrate just how big it is, imagine this: with the money made in human trafficking every year, you could buy every Starbucks franchise in the world, every

OLD SLAVERY VERSUS NEW SLAVERY

Slave (n): "a person who is the property of and wholly subject to another."

Though the definition fits both historic transatlantic slavery and modern-day slavery, there are differences that make it problematic to draw overly general or simplistic parallels and applications. For example:

—Old slavery existed as the protected law of the land, making its practice open and overt; new slavery functions outside of the law and is perpetuated by criminals or criminal organizations, making its practice hidden and often difficult to discover.

—Old slavery was founded in deep hate and racial discrimination and politics; new slavery is for the most part based on profit and opportunity rather than race and policy.

—The effects of old slavery didn't necessarily go away with its legal abolition (for example, "freed" slaves in the British West Indies often were forced into indentured servitude instead, and "freed" slaves in America were often left destitute and without opportunity or hope, a societal effect that still has lingering consequences today). Therefore, applying "solutions" from the "success" of old abolitionism may prove overly simplistic and less applicable, as "success" is a difficult thing to quantify.

—Both old slavery and new slavery put their victims in the worst imaginable positions. One form cannot easily be judged as being more difficult or severe than the other.

NBA team in the nation, and every Target store across the globe. With millions of women and children being sold each year for sex, labor, and organ harvesting, this is an epidemic of the worst kind.[1] Indeed, we must do all we can to improve our effectiveness in this fight. And so we must not, we cannot, ignore the lessons of history.

I won't attempt to identify overly general applications and parallels between the old slavery and the new, particularly those that can't be specifically backed up. Instead, I will simply tell you my personal story of discovery and application. That story will show that, for me, nineteenth-century rescue and restoration missions have been directly responsible for many of the modern-day equivalents that I have personally participated in.

This is why I chose to name my foundation—whose mission is to rescue and restore victims of modern-day slavery, and to see that slave captors are prosecuted to the fullest extent of the law— Operation Underground Railroad.

The name choice came naturally to me, as I had become attached to historical efforts to combat slavery very early in my career. When I was asked by my employer, Homeland Security Investigations (an agency of the Department of Homeland Security), to help start a child crimes/ countertrafficking group in the early to mid 2000s, very little was known about modern-day slavery, particularly as it concerned children. The press was almost silent about it, and governments of the world were just tuning in to how big it really was. The United States led the way by initiating efforts like the Internet Crimes Against Children Task Force, of which I quickly became a member. But even those task forces were pretty new and still trying to wrap their collective arms around the problem.

When I was sent to undercover operator school to learn how

to infiltrate child-trafficking rings, I realized how new our countermeasures really were. There was little in the way of curriculum for infiltrating this particular crime. In fact, I remember being a bit startled during one of my first simulation exercises in undercover school. I was sitting across the table from one of my undercover instructors, who was playing the role of a criminal smuggler, and I began to engage him in a conversation about how I might purchase children for sex on the black market. My stomach hurt as I brought up the subject, but I fought through it. About two minutes into the exercise, my instructor went silent and turned pale. He stood up from the table and said, "I can't do this. I have a baby daughter." Then he walked out of the room, thus ending the simulation exercise.

Another experienced instructor came up to me and put his hand on my shoulder. "Tim," he said, "we are going to have to pioneer this one."

It wasn't that my agency was uncaring. To the contrary. They began pouring all sorts of resources into this problem, and today they lead the world in countertrafficking measures. It's just that, when I was starting, the severity of the problem was just being discovered. Fortunately, I had the best agency and best team I could ask for, as we all entered the darkness together.

I also had *history.* Lacking any other instruction manual on the subject of modern-day slavery, I turned to history in quiet desperation. I bought every book I could on the transatlantic slave trade, on the Civil War, on Abraham Lincoln, and on the Underground Railroad.

I learned that "Underground Railroad" was the name given to a secret network of undercover operators, safe houses, transports, and routes that facilitated the rescue and escape of thousands of nineteenth-century slaves from slave territories (like Harriet

Jacobs's North Carolina and other Southern states) to free territories (like New York, Massachusetts, Canada, and even Mexico). The loosely organized and administered network was established in the late 1700s and grew until the Civil War ended the wicked slave practice once and for all.

In the end, I realized that if we could make honest connections between the transatlantic slave trade and modern-day slavery, two things would happen. First, we would shine a light on that tragic era of American history so as to ensure it would never be forgotten. Second, we would have some sort of map from this history in order to help us deal with slavery today. And by map, I'm not only talking about the inspiration to move forward. As you will see later in this book, the abolitionist movement and the Underground Railroad also provided me and O.U.R. with tactical ideas that have informed our strategy in planning undercover rescue operations, helped us deal with the politics of modern-day slavery, and guided us in our efforts to rehabilitate and restore broken lives.

As Coach Tomlin pointed out in his Foreword, when I began conversing with him on the subject, I realized there were other, more unusual elements of this sacred history that could help us in our fight today. Again, very few groups prior to the Civil War were able to drop their hate, divisiveness, biases, and prejudices to work together on much of anything; yet, the Underground Railroad did exactly that by focusing on something bigger than any one individual. That thing was people in captivity. That thing was children being mercilessly abused and exploited. Though the network was often disorganized and, as with any organization built under such stress, though its members argued about how to run it best, yet they came together: black, white, and every other color and creed. They embraced each other and by so doing

HARRIET TUBMAN AND THE UNDERGROUND RAILROAD

Born Araminta Ross, Harriet Tubman (1822–1911) was severely beaten and abused as a child slave in Maryland. Relying on her faith in God, she eventually connected to elements of the Underground Railroad, which helped her escape slavery and make it safely to the Northern states. Once safe in her freedom, she risked it all by becoming one of the greatest operators on the very Underground Railroad that had rescued her. Carrying her trademark pistol, she conducted thirteen rescue operations into the South to liberate captives and bring them to safety. She became famous for going undercover in the South, using various disguises in order to reach and rescue the captive. She even placed certain codes into a song, "Go Down, Moses," in order to give messages to her people to prepare them for their escape. Because of her faith, her love of the Old Testament, and her willingness to risk her very life to guide her people to freedom, she was given the nickname "Moses."

When the Civil War broke out, Tubman worked for the Union army as a nurse and as an armed scout and spy. She was the first woman to lead an armed expedition in the war, during the raid at Combahee Ferry, which liberated nearly 700 slaves.

produced a needed light in their dark world. They took that light, joined hands, and walked together into the darkness to liberate the innocent, suffering, and helpless children of God.[2] Certainly there are lessons for us here today.

On so many levels, we needed to resurrect certain elements of history. Hence the name *Operation Underground Railroad*. In the original Underground Railroad, there were many players, and many organizations, working separately and together (when possible) for the common cause. The same can be said of rescue and rehabilitation efforts and organizations today. We honor them all. And we stand shoulder to shoulder with any person or group willing to fight this fight.

◆　◆　◆

With that background, I want to return to Harriet Jacobs. Before we get into the body of this book, which will share many particulars of her shocking, almost unbelievable life story, I want to further explain why she, more than all the others (including the more well-known historical players), piqued my interest and became my personal hero of heroes. For one thing, she attacked the problem of slavery from every angle. While some (like Harriet Tubman) found historical fame for their daring rescue operations, others (like Frederick Douglass) were known for their influence in speaking and writing, and still others (like Abraham Lincoln) exhibited political genius, Harriet Jacobs participated bravely, passionately, and effectively in all these aspects.

As we will see throughout this book, she was a rescuer in her own right, she wrote one of the most important books on slavery in her time, she fought the political fight, and she did something else. Something that makes her unique, in my eyes. She was a healer. In fact, that seemed to be her emphasis in the fight: to seek out the innocent fugitive, the downtrodden, the abused, and nurse them back to health and happiness. And her focus was the children who had been victimized by the demon called slavery. For us today, the healing and restoration is the most important part of the rescue, and Harriet (as you will see) continues to be our guide in those efforts.

And yet there is more. The deeper I dig into American slavery, the more surprised I become by how much of the narrative has been left out of the history—or at least what most people know of that history. When American slavery is considered, generally visions of innocent and tortured people of African descent toiling away on Southern plantations sums it up. That was bad enough, to be sure. But there were darker layers. There was sex slavery, too. Sex trafficking. Perhaps students of history haven't wanted to focus too much attention on this aspect, as it hurts too much. But we need to consider it in order to honor black history. We also need to consider it because there are parallels to modern-day sex slavery and trafficking. As the focus of O.U.R. is to fight modern-day sex slavery, we seek to learn from this history. And Harriet Jacobs, perhaps more than any other, teaches us. For her story, which she bravely told in her autobiography, *Incidents in the Life of a Slave Girl,* focuses our attention on the sex slavery of the nineteenth century. (Quotations from her book, hereafter cited as *ILSG,* appear throughout this volume.)

Of all the stories connected to Harriet that have drawn me to her, I have yet to mention the most important one, at least to me. Unless you understand this one, the rest of this book will not make sense.

To really introduce you to this particular story and its deep connection to my interests, I need to take you to Edenton, North Carolina, the town where Harriet toiled away under the dark

IDENTIFYING THE TRUE HARRIET

In order to protect those in the South who had broken laws to help her escape, Harriet wrote her book, *Incidents in the Life of a Slave Girl,* using the name Linda Brent. She also changed the names of other people and places in her book. Though many in her abolitionist circles knew it was her, and though many read her book at the time, her identity as the author was soon lost to later generations. In fact, until recently, modern scholars, who could not verify the existence of a Linda Brent, believed her book to be a work of fiction written by zealous nineteenth-century abolitionists. This is one reason her book never achieved modern-day fame as it should have and why the name Harriet Jacobs has not generally been listed among the most recognizable names of nineteenth-century abolitionism, as it most as-suredly deserves to be. It wasn't until a modern-day professor, Jean Fagan Yellin, began putting the puzzle together that the story was verified as being absolutely true. In 2004, Professor Yellin published her book *Harriet Jacobs: A Life,* thus reintroducing Harriet to the world at large and bringing to life the story of a true American heroine.

cloud of human captivity. Surprisingly, the town hasn't modernized all that much, allowing visitors today to see and feel something of what Harriet did. I have made multiple trips to the town, exploring where Harriet lived, walking over the streets where she walked, sitting in the places where she hid, where she cried, and where she prayed. But of all the historical sites in Edenton, there is one that reflects this important story more than any other. It is the county jail—a small, two-story brick building that is now condemned but was alive and well during Harriet's day, back when the dark cloud of slavery filled the streets of Edenton.

I have always had a strange fascination with jails. Actually, it is a mix of fascination and fear. As a special agent for the United States government, I had arrested many people (mostly sex traffickers and pedophiles) and taken them to jail. Of course, those people deserved to be there, but the idea of someone being held captive somewhere, anywhere, deeply bothered me. The thought made me feel claustrophobic. Panicky. When visiting these jails, I would always picture what it would be like to be falsely imprisoned. Whenever my work took me there, I would always get out as fast as possible. I remember thinking, as I exited those dark buildings, how badly I wanted to just go home and hug my wife and kids.

The county jail in Edenton was fifty times more fascinating and a hundred times more frightening than any other jail I had ever visited. For this jail had not always been used for just purposes. (Slavery absolutely corrupts those institutions designed to serve and protect.) It had been a tool of wickedness used against many innocent people. Two of those innocent people sentenced to this jail were Harriet's own children, six-year-old Joseph and two-year-old Louisa (or "Lulu"). It was their story that brought me closer to Harriet than anything else.

After serving their "sentence" of about two months, the children were taken from the jail. They were thrown into a horse-drawn carriage where other slaves sat restrained, their arms, both right and left, handcuffed to a single chain running the length of the carriage. The group, along with the children, had been purchased by a slave trader, and they were being transported to their new homes and new masters.

As the carriage pulled away from the jail and out of town, Joseph and Lulu spotted their great-grandmother Molly, who had brought what clothes she could find for their new lives on some plantation under the rule of some master far, far away. Nobody was allowed to know where the trafficked men, women, and children were going to be taken. Seeing the children being trafficked away was too much for Grandma Molly. She fainted and collapsed in the street. "And now came the trying hour," as Harriet would later describe this scene, "for the drove of human beings, driven away like cattle, to be sold they knew not where. Husbands were torn from wives, parents from children, never to look upon each other again this side of the grave. There was wringing of hands and cries of despair" (*ILSG*, 137).

As I have thought over this scene and hundreds just like it, my mind can't fully process it all. How can humans be so brutal to each other, especially to children? How does a society get to such a dark place? And what can be done about it? It wasn't just curiosity that compelled me to ask these questions. It wasn't just my interest in history, either. Rather, it was my interest in the present, for I knew two other children, about the same age as Harriet's, who had been living almost parallel lives. Slavery. *Modern-day* slavery. Their names are Mia and Marky—also sister and brother—and as babies born in the island nation of Haiti, they had joined the ranks of the millions of other children in the world to be enslaved.[3] Abused. Trafficked.

While studying the life of Harriet and her children, I had simultaneously been working feverishly with the Haitian police to infiltrate the trafficking ring that held Mia and Marky. I took my first trip to Edenton during this difficult time. I went to seek inspiration and knowledge, to learn at the feet of Harriet Jacobs. Harriet had done something I wanted to do. She had freed those children. *That* was why I had come to Edenton. *That* was why I connected so powerfully to Harriet.

On this first trip to Edenton, I brought my twelve-year-old daughter, Anne, with me to take photographs. Once in Edenton, our first stop was, of course, the county jail. It was instantly the symbol for me of the slavery I was combating at that very time, Joseph and Lulu becoming emblematic of Mia and Marky. The closer I got to Harriet's and her children's story, the closer I would get to the answers I needed. And it seemed there was no place I could go to get closer to the story than right into the jail itself.

En route to the jail, Anne and I came to a large and elegant lawn lined with large trees, which led its visitors up a hill to the county courthouse. The structure, built in 1767, was still there and still looking as it had in Harriet's day. My heart began beating faster as we walked up the lawn toward the courthouse; I knew the jail was just behind the old structure.

Anne and I took a deep breath. We then walked around to the back of the courthouse, our hearts beating heavy and fast in anticipation. As we rounded the corner, a most frightening sight stopped me dead in my tracks. There was a pillory—a whipping post. It was only a replica, but I had studied what had happened at this very spot, "just at the back of the court-house and in front

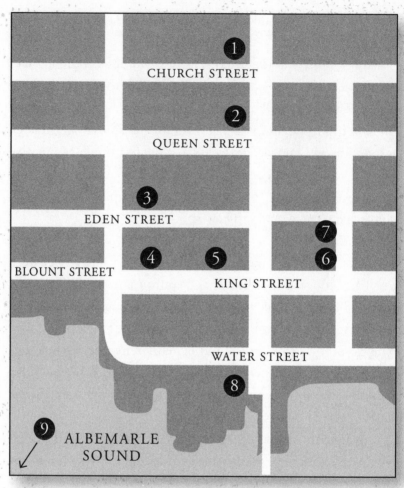

CHURCH STREET

QUEEN STREET

EDEN STREET

BLOUNT STREET

KING STREET

WATER STREET

ALBEMARLE
SOUND

*Map of Edenton, North Carolina, identifying
important places in the life of Harriet Jacobs*

1. St. Paul's Episcopal Church
2. Martha Blount's home
3. Dr. James Norcom's home
4. Samuel Tradwell Sawyer's home
5. Molly Horniblow's home
6. Chowan County Courthouse
7. Chowan County Jail
8. Edenton Bay Harbor / Maritime Underground Railroad Site
9. Snaky Swamp

Courthouse in Edenton, North Carolina

of the jail," as one nineteenth-century eyewitness had described the small space of horror. I could see in my mind's eye the blood dripping down and pooling at the feet of the innocent slave victims tied to the post. I could hear in my mind's ear the screaming, the despair.

I pushed the images out of my mind and looked beyond the massacre, though I knew I would have to come back to it eventually. Working as an undercover operator in the dark world of human slavery for over a decade, I had learned how to see horrific images and somehow push them out for the time being so I could focus on the task at hand.

I could do it, but I didn't want Anne to think too much. So I employed my emotional defenses and turned our attention to the little brick building beyond the pillory.

The jail, of course, wasn't necessarily a happy thought for either of us, but it wasn't as bad as the death scene we had just walked through. I needed to break the silence for my own well-being, but especially for Anne.

"I wish so badly we could go inside the jail," I whispered to Anne.

"Maybe we can!" she replied. "I prayed for it, remember?"

She had. That morning at breakfast, the owner of our hotel (a bed-and-breakfast converted from an old Southern plantation home) had told us that the old jail, being a condemned building, was locked shut and even had a nail driven through the door and into the frame to make sure nobody passed its threshold. After breakfast we had returned to our room, and I had heard Anne pray that somehow the door would be opened for us. She knew how badly I wanted to get in.

Walking beyond the pillory, we approached the front of the jail. Small. Simple. Lonely looking. A small sign stated that the jail was built in 1825. *If only its walls could talk,* I thought to myself.

"Dad! Look!" Anne yelled excitedly, shattering the renewed silence that had accompanied our short walk from the pillory toward the jail.

"The door is open!" she continued as she ran ahead of me, darting toward the jail door.

As I approached the door, all I could do was smile. I was speechless. The door *was* open just a crack, unlocked and unrestrained. The large nail was still in the door, angled toward the door frame and poking out the back. But it was inches away from where it had been, where it was supposed to be, inserted into the frame. It was as if some very strong person had come over and yanked the door back, ripping the nail out of the door frame. I ran my finger along the empty nail hole as I cautiously pushed on the door, looking around to make sure nobody was watching. There was no sign indicating it was unlawful to enter, but it

The door of the jail

still felt kind of like trespassing. I looked at Anne, thought of her prayer that morning, and knew I had no choice.

I used my foot to kick the door the rest of the way open. It was time to get our hands dirty. It was time to enter this dark narrative, knowing there would eventually be light at the end of the tunnel.

I took Anne's hand. We stepped in.

CHAPTER 1

EDENTON, NORTH CAROLINA, 1813

Harriet Jacobs was born in 1813 in Edenton, North Carolina, to her slave mother, Delilah, daughter of Molly Horniblow, and her slave father, a carpenter named Elijah. Harriet was blessed with one brother, two years younger than she. His name was John, and he would be her best friend for life. Harriet, John, and their family were never supposed to have been slaves. They fell into it due to the circumstances of the times in which they lived: namely, the American Revolution.

Harriet's grandmother, Molly, was a child during that war. Though Molly's family had been born into slavery, when their master had died, he had willed them all free and provided them money to help them in their freedom. Molly and her family boarded a boat to take them away. But with war vessels, chaos, and suspicion all about, the boat was seized. Molly and her family were unsuccessful in convincing officials of their emancipation. Greed set in, and the family members were sold to different buyers.

Molly ended up in Edenton, property of the Horniblow family. She was made to work in the Horniblows' tavern and hotel, which stood next door to Edenton's courthouse and jail. There she toiled for years. But the Horniblow family eventually saw her strong work ethic, her intelligence, and her bright spirit. They grew to love and respect her, at least as much as white slaveholders could. They granted her request to employ herself after-hours as a baker. She began saving money so that she might one day purchase her five children, whom she had been raising in Edenton. One of those children was Delilah, mother of young Harriet and little John.

Harriet was naturally born into slavery, also property of the Horniblow family. But Harriet was not treated as a slave. In fact, as a child she might not have even known she was a slave. She lived a happy childhood with her mother and father. Her mother died when she was only six. She was then sent to live with her mother's mistress, an unwed Horniblow daughter named Margaret. Margaret loved Harriet and treated her well. She taught Harriet to read, write, and sew—highly unusual skills for a slave. "I loved her," Harriet later wrote, "for she had been almost like a mother to me" (*ILSG*, 8).

But then Margaret died. Harriet was twelve years old, and her life would never be the same.

Margaret had promised Harriet's mother that the young girl would never suffer. So naturally, Harriet, also knowing how Margaret loved her, believed that Margaret would have kept her word and emancipated her in her final will. It's possible that Margaret intended to do so. But strangely, Margaret's will kept Harriet enslaved. Stranger still, Margaret never signed the will.

Here's what we know: As Margaret lay dying, the town doctor was called. This doctor happened to be married to Margaret's sister, Mary Matilda. His name was James Norcom, and in the coming chapters you will see him for the vile and merciless antagonist he would become in Harriet's story. Margaret's written deathbed will and testament bequeathed twelve-year-old Harriet to Dr. Norcom's three-year-old daughter (also named Mary Matilda). In other words, Harriet was now under the power and control of Dr.

Norcom. As I said, Margaret never signed the will, but Dr. James Norcom, standing in as witness, certainly did!

Perhaps Harriet's grandma Molly could help. Perhaps she could somehow intervene. With Harriet's mother and now her mistress both dead, Grandma Molly was Harriet's last hope. But Molly was facing problems of her own. Her own mistress had also been ill, and she had died shortly after Margaret did. By all accounts, the mistress's will had set Molly free, but when the estate was settled, something mysteriously changed, and Molly was sent to be sold on the auction block. The mystery was again tied to the mistress's son-in-law, James Norcom.

Dr. Norcom broke the news to Molly, telling her that she would not be set free, but sold. He also told her that, due to her committed service and the love the mistress had always felt for her, he would spare her the indignity of being sold at public auction. But that was another trick. He feared there would be an outcry should Molly be sold publicly, for the townspeople knew and loved her. They endearingly called her "Aunt Molly," and they knew she was supposed to be emancipated. Norcom wanted to keep his evil deed hidden, but Molly saw through his scheming. She insisted on taking her place on the auction block.

As she stood on the block, chattel to be sold, not a single offer came in. Instead, different shouts came forth. "'Shame! Shame!' the crowd cried, 'Who is going to sell you Aunt [Molly]? Don't stand there! That is no place for *you*'" (*ILSG*, 13). Finally a hand raised. It was the seventy-year-old sister of the recently deceased mistress. She knew the truth and chose to do the right thing. She offered fifty dollars, and nobody dared outbid her. Upon purchasing Molly, the elderly, feeble woman immediately went to the courthouse and legally set her free (*ILSG*, 14).

Grandma Molly purchased a small home on King Street,

me or to which I may be in any manner entitled.

And I hereby nominate
and appoint my friend Doct. James
Norcom Executor of this my last
will and testament. In testimony
of which I have hereunto set my
hand and Seal the eighth day
of April 1825

Witness   Margaret Horniblow   {Seal}
Wm M Jones
Henry Flury Junr

Codicil; It is my will & desire that
the foregoing devise be so far altered, that
my negro girl Harriet be given to my niece
Mary Matilda Norcom Daughter of Dr James Norcom;
and I further give & bequeath to my said niece
my Bureau & work table & their contents —

The above Codicil was
acknoliged before us the 3 day of July
the year above wrote

Henry Flury.

Jno Norcom.

Deathbed codicil forcing Harriet to remain a slave

which doubled as her bakery. There she built up her business, and she did not want for customers. One block away was Eden Street—the place where sat the Norcom residence. Grandma Molly's precious Harriet was now toiling away in that home. Norcom had also purchased Harriet's brother, John, who would work as his medical assistant at his practice.

So there they were. In many ways, it was going to play out like a chess game, with Grandma Molly on one end and Dr. James Norcom on the other. And the queen whose movements were watched and obsessed over by both sides was Harriet Jacobs.

Grandma made a move. She bought a new pair of shoes for her slave granddaughter on Eden Street. The Norcoms countered. They couldn't have Harriet so easily be the recipient of someone else's generosity. That might make her believe she was something more than the family's property. Mrs. Norcom complained of the noise the shoes made as Harriet walked, so Harriet was forced to take her shoes and socks off. She was then forced to run an errand for the master that required her to walk a long distance outdoors in the ice and snow. And she had to do it barefoot. She would learn her lesson. By the time Harriet returned, she was ill. "I went to bed [that night] thinking the next day would find me sick, perhaps dead," Harriet later recalled. "What was my grief on waking to find myself quite well!" (*ILSG,* 23).

The reality of slavery was setting in. A dark world she had not yet known in her life began hovering over her, getting darker and darker by the day. And she was about to be thrust deeper into the hellacious darkness.

"I shall never forget that night," Harriet wrote. She had been on Eden Street for only a few weeks when it happened. A slave had been brought to the Norcoms' Eden Street property from the Norcom plantation miles outside of town. Master Norcom

Bond of emanicipation for Molly Horniblow, grandmother of Harriet Jacobs ordered the slave to be tied up to the joist of his workhouse in such a manner that his feet dangled just above the ground. Master Norcom then calmly took his tea. When he was done, Norcom entered the workhouse and came face to face with the slave. "Never before, in my life," Harriet wrote, "had I heard hundreds of blows fall, in succession, on a human being. His piteous groans, and his 'O, pray don't, massa,' rang in my ears for months afterwards" (*ILSG*, 15).

But when Harriet learned exactly why the man had been beaten so badly—*that* was when it really struck her to the core. That was when it became more threatening to her personally as a young girl.

As it turned out, the man's wife, also a slave, had recently given birth. When the baby was delivered, the evidence was out—he was not the father. The baby was white. The child had been fathered by Master Norcom. The slave husband was irate and made public his hurtful discovery. As punishment, he was beaten, then later, both he and his wife were sold. "You have let

James Norcom

Dr. Norcom's Eden Street home

your tongue run too far; damn you!" Norcom said to the new mother as she was carted away by the slave trader (*ILSG*, 16).

Harriet would soon witness a similar case. A young slave girl, having just given birth to a white child, lay dying after complications from the delivery. The dying girl's mother, also a slave, sat grieving by her side. The mistress of the home, instead of pointing blame at her husband, blamed the innocent young girl. "You suffer, do you?," the mistress squealed, "I'm glad of it. You deserve it all, and more too."

The dying girl's mother then declared, "The baby is dead, thank God; and I hope my poor child will soon be in heaven, too." The mistress shot back, "Heaven! There is no such place for the like of her and her bastard." All the slave mother could do was sob over her girl.

"Don't grieve so, mother;" the sickly girl whispered to her sobbing mother, having heard the sharp and hurtful words of the mistress. "God knows all about it;" the girl continued, hoping to comfort her mother, "and HE will have mercy upon me." The young girl, who had just watched her baby pass away, followed that baby to heaven shortly thereafter. The slave mother thanked God that her daughter and grandbaby had escaped this dark mortality (*ILSG*, 16).

Young Harriet knew what was coming. The writing was on the wall. She had identified at least eleven slave children as the biological children of James Norcom (*ILSG*, 43).

Eventually it started. In Harriet's words, Norcom "tried his utmost to corrupt the pure principles my grandmother had instilled. He peopled my young mind with unclean images, such as only a vile monster could think of. I turned from him with disgust and hatred. But he was my master. I was compelled to live under the same roof with him—where I saw a man forty years my senior daily violating the most sacred commandments of nature. He told me I was his property; that I must be subject to his will in all things."

Harriet did all that she could to avoid him. But where could she go? To whom could she turn for protection? "My master met me at every turn," explained Harriet, "reminding me that I belonged to him, and swearing by heaven and earth that he would compel me to submit to him. If I went out for a breath of fresh air, after a day of unwearied toil, his footsteps dogged me. If I knelt by my mother's grave, his dark shadow fell on me even there" (*ILSG*, 35).

The other slaves saw the struggle. They saw what danger the innocent adolescent girl was being led into. Though Harriet had, by nature, a very "light heart," she now became "heavy with sad forebodings." Harriet wanted to talk to someone about it—she desired someone to confide in. But everybody at the Norcom estate "knew too well the guilty practices under that roof; and they were aware that to speak of them was an offense that never went unpunished." Harriet thought to confide in Grandma Molly. But Norcom had assured her of the consequences: the master "swore he would kill me," wrote Harriet, "if I was not as silent as the grave" (*ILSG*, 35).

What would Harriet do? Would she fight back? Would anyone come to help? Would she escape? How?

CHAPTER 2

PORT-AU-PRINCE, HAITI, 2010

wish this part were fiction. But it's not.

Just before 5:00 p.m. on January 12, 2010, a 7.0-magnitude earthquake hit the island nation of Haiti. Immediate and immense death and destruction followed. The Presidential Palace and National Assembly building collapsed, along with the UN Stabilization Mission headquarters, killing the UN Mission chief. More than a million people were instantly displaced, and more than 200,000 were dead. Thousands of people had suddenly become widows, widowers, and orphans.

A young girl named Mia, who could not have been more than three years old, and her brother, Marky, likely under two years old, were among those instantly orphaned.[4]

Fortunately for little Marky, Mia was a special girl. Mature for her age, she had always been Marky's best friend. Now she was all he had. She would have to do her best to become his mother.

Somehow the two children survived when their cement house in Port-au-Prince (Haiti's capital) collapsed, killing the rest of their family. Mia did not know what to do or where to go. She took Marky's hand and began to walk. Such a scene I can't imagine. With bodies dotting the landscape—blood, terror, smoke, and chaos all about—these children walked. Lost. Frightened. They aimlessly meandered through it all, waiting, watching, hoping.

According to the official report issued by Haiti's Child Welfare Service, a kind face eventually appeared through the dust and mayhem. An elderly woman. By all accounts, a good woman, though nobody knows who she was or where she went afterward. She took the children by the hand and escorted them to the only place she could think of that might be able to help. It was an orphanage—at least that was what the words painted on the cinderblock walls of the compound indicated. And it had survived the quake. Maybe someone inside the place could care for the children.

She approached the gate and was met by a middle-aged woman, presumably the keeper of the place. The madam of the house. The madam received the children and promised to take care of them. Mia and Marky entered.

The elderly woman walked away, as satisfied as she could be, considering the circumstances. If only she knew what she had just done.

On that same day, not far from where Mia and Marky had been taken, another little girl, no more than about nine years old, pulled herself from the rubble of what had been her home. Her name was Rosi, and she too had just joined the ranks of Haiti's hosts of orphans. Driven by hunger and desperation, Rosi left her parents' lifeless bodies in search of succor. Before long she was approached by a concerned-looking stranger who offered her something to eat and a place to stay. With nowhere else to go, Rosi followed the stranger. Little did she know that she had fallen into a foul trap, a den of nightmares that would hold her hostage for the next eight years.

The moment Mia, Marky, and Rosi crossed the thresholds of their traffickers' lairs, they were on the auction block. They were now for sale to anyone. They were available to be purchased and used for whatever nefarious purpose evil minds could conjure up.

These stories (at least the vague facts about them we can find) have played out in my mind hundreds of times over several years as I have sought to put all the details together. How on earth did I become attached to these stories in the first place? How could I have ever entered such an obscure narrative, about such obscure children, living in such an obscure nation? Even now, it's astonishing to me. Truth be told, when I heard about the earthquake I (shamefully) thought little of it. I was busy raising my children along with my wife, Katherine, and working as a special agent for the U.S. Department of Homeland Security. I was stationed in Calexico, California, right on the border with Mexico. When I heard the news of the devastating earthquake, I knew virtually nothing about Haiti and didn't care to. Like I said, I was very busy. But nowadays, not a day goes by that I'm not thinking, planning, or scheming about some initiative, project, or operation connected to the island nation.

But why? How? The link between me and Haiti (and, more important, to Mia, Marky, and Rosi) begins with a parallel narrative, which was taking place during the same hours that the three children were walking the streets of a broken Port-au-Prince in the quake's aftermath. This parallel narrative is about another Haitian child: Gardy Mardy. He was barely three years old when the quake struck. Somehow, some way, little Gardy ended up at the same false orphanage as Mia and Marky, under the care of the same wicked madam. Did Mia and Marky see Gardy? Did they know each other? Did they cross paths? These are questions I have yet to answer.

One day, not long after the quake, Gardy's story landed in a small news article that came across my online news feed. I can't remember how I ended up seeing it. Perhaps someone sent it to me. Though it certainly affected me, I didn't immediately think too much about it. My work as a government agent exposed me to horrific stories every day. I had learned to push through it all and get back to normal pretty quick.

But there was something about the story that particularly haunted me. It was a picture of Gardy's father, Guesno Mardy. The photo depicted him removing rubble and helping the injured in Port-au-Prince. He buried family members after the quake and almost lost his wife. All this happened while he was searching for his baby son, Gardy, who had been kidnapped and trafficked just a few weeks before the quake, on December 6. The picture of Guesno wouldn't leave me alone. *How could anyone possibly endure so much at once?* After a couple of weeks of trying to shake it, I couldn't go on. I reached out to Guesno, and he responded. And my world was changed forever.

I will eventually tell you the whole story about Mia, Marky, Gardy, and Guesno. But before I get too far ahead of myself, let's back up and discuss the bigger picture here. Today, there are

Guesno Mardy

approximately twenty to thirty million people enslaved. Close to six million of these modern-day slave victims are children.[5] Human trafficking brings in an estimated 150 billion dollars annually and is the fastest growing criminal enterprise on the planet.[6] With thousands of children currently forced into the commercial sex trade in the United States,[7] and thousands more children smuggled into the U.S. annually for the same purpose, this problem is never far from home. It's everywhere.

Haiti is especially troubling. As the poorest nation in the Western Hemisphere,[8] it lacks the resources (such as strong law enforcement and solid educational opportunities) that might otherwise protect children from the evils of trafficking and slavery. Haiti is also home to close to half a million *Restaveks,* children who are sent away from their families, generally due to impoverished conditions, to work as "domestic servants" of others who have the means to provide for their needs. Though culturally accepted by many, this system can quickly become a form of slavery. Abuse usually follows, often sexual abuse. I have seen it with my own eyes again and again. Conditions such as these have led Haiti to continually receive some of the lowest classifications possible on the United States Trafficking in Persons Report.[9] It is a mess! Without aggressive intervention, trafficking and abuse quickly become the future for children like Mia, Marky, Rosi, and Gardy.

CHAPTER 3

EDENTON, NORTH CAROLINA, CIRCA 1827

At the time Dr. Norcom began pursuing young Harriet with lewd proposals, there was no easily accessible Underground Railroad route for her. She almost certainly would have known about Snaky Swamp, the island marshlands that sat across the bay from Edenton, whose miles of dense forest, waterways, and swamps would eventually become a renowned refuge along the Underground Railroad. The perfect hiding place. Harriet would one day use it herself to escape slavery.

But for now, young Harriet was not prepared to make her escape. Yet she was also not prepared to allow her master to overpower her. She decided to take courage, to begin her fight against him.

Her efforts began simply. First, she played dumb. When Norcom propositioned her, she acted as though she were too young to understand his meaning, then carried on with her duties as if nothing had happened. Harriet's aunt Betty, daughter of Grandma Molly, was also a slave in the Norcom home. Betty loved Harriet and was very sympathetic to her situation. Harriet took extra precautions by making sure to sleep every night next to her aunt, thus deterring Norcom from attempting to violate her (*ILSG*, 39–40).

Norcom responded by putting his baby daughter in his own private room to sleep with him every night. This gave him the excuse to ask Harriet to sleep near her (really near him!) to act as "nurse" to the child. Harriet responded by leveling up her own game. She decided to involve Norcom's wife in the conversation. Harriet bravely told her everything, how her husband had been preying upon her and how she had been denying every advance. Instead of pity, jealousy ensued in Mrs. Norcom. She now hated Harriet for her own husband's crimes. Mrs. Norcom demanded that the slave girl sleep in *her* private room, where she could watch her. As difficult as it was for Harriet to be the constant subject of Mrs. Norcom's jealousy and wrath for the rest of their lives, at least the plan had worked in other respects. James Norcom had been caught, and his wife was now watching him like a hawk (*ILSG*, 42–43).

IN HARRIET'S WORDS

"Slavery is a curse to the whites as well as to the blacks. It makes the white fathers cruel and sensual; the sons violent and licentious; it contaminates the daughters, and makes the wives wretched" (*ILSG*, 66).

Harriet made her next move. She was determined to exercise the rights she was born with as a human being and as a daughter of God. She allowed herself to fall in love with a kind man, a black carpenter, who was free. The man eventually asked for her hand in marriage. Harriet was so excited. She said yes, but, knowing she was considered Norcom's property by law, she knew she had to get his permission.

Because Mrs. Norcom hated her so, Harriet hoped the family would agree to sell her to her lover, who was more than willing to buy Harriet's freedom. Harriet decided to ask a friend, a trusted white woman in town, to approach James Norcom first with the idea. Shortly after the proposition reached him, he called Harriet into his office. She did not know what to expect.

Mary Norcom

"So you want to be married, do you?" he said.

"Yes, sir," Harriet responded.

Norcom said he would not allow it, but that she could marry one of his slaves if she must be married.

Harriet took a measure of courage and stood up for herself. "Do you suppose, sir, that a slave can have some preference about marrying? Do you suppose that all men are alike to her?"

Norcom's eyes intensified. He wasn't used to a slave questioning him.

"Do you love this nigger?" he asked.

"Yes, sir," was the immediate reply.

"How dare you tell me so," Norcom shot back, angry because she had chosen a black man over him. Norcom was furious and began insulting Harriet's lover, calling him a "puppy," which was his way of trying to convince her she was in love with someone less than human.

"If he is a puppy I am a puppy," Harriet struck back, "for we are both of the negro race. It is right and honorable for us to love each other."

Again, Norcom was unaccustomed to having a slave lecture him. But Harriet wasn't done yet. She was about to go for the jugular.

"The man you call a puppy," she said, "never insulted me."

By indirectly referencing Norcom, who insulted Harriet constantly, she had placed the two men side by side and ranked them against each other. And Norcom came in *below* the "puppy."

Harriet described what happened next: "He sprang upon me like a tiger, and gave me a stunning blow."

That kind of violence had always worked before. Harriet was supposed to now follow her script and immediately apologize and succumb.

But she didn't.

She stood up and declared, "You have struck me for answering you honestly. How I despise you!"

Norcom didn't know what to do with this. His strategy to subdue her was failing. So he upped the ante.

"Do you know that I have a right to do as I like with you,—that I might kill you if I please?"

"You have tried to kill me," Harriet responded, "and I wish you had; but you have no right to do as you like with me."

Desperate, Norcom sought another form of punishment that might scare her into submission. As her owner, he had the legal right to send her to the county jail.

"How would you like to be sent to jail for your insolence?" he threatened.

"As for the jail," she retorted, "there would be more peace for me there than there is here."

Harriet truly believed that, as she would prove later. And the defeated Norcom must have believed her, as he quickly rescinded his offer to send her there.

Not knowing what else to do, Norcom forbade Harriet from seeing her fiancé, and threatened to kill the man should he set foot on his property.

Though Harriet did see her fiancé again, and was beaten again by Norcom for doing so, ultimately she made a decision. Were she to marry the man she loved and have children, she realized that the children would by law belong to Norcom. Norcom's special hatred of the man who had won Harriet's affections—the man to whom he had lost in that way—would undoubtedly be manifested in vengeful acts over the innocent children. Harriet loved her man too much to subject him to watching his children be abused by such evil. She told him to leave Edenton, to move to the free states, and to never come back. "For *his* sake," Harriet explained, "I felt that I ought not to link his fate with my own unhappy destiny." He sorrowfully did as she requested. Harriet

UNDERGROUND TEACHER: HARRIET FIGHTS AGAINST THE SYSTEM

In 1830, the state of North Carolina made a law "to prevent all persons from teaching Slaves to read and write."[10] Most states in the Southern United States had similar laws. An elderly slave named "Uncle Fred" asked Harriet to teach him to read. Harriet reminded him that they could both be whipped and imprisoned should Harriet give him lessons. They both decided it was worth the risk. "Honey," old Uncle Fred told Harriet while holding up a copy of the Bible, "it 'pears when I can read dis good book I shall be nearer to God. . . . I only wants to read dis book, dat I may know how to live; den I hab no fear 'bout dying" (*ILSG*, 94).

was left alone. "The lamp of hope had gone out," she explained. "The dream of my girlhood was over" (*ILSG*, 47–53).

With Harriet's fiancé out of the picture, Norcom struck again. He tried a different approach—slyly, deceptively trying to play a "romantic" angle. He told her he had begun to build a small cottage on his land miles outside of town. Harriet would live in the cottage, without having to toil as a labor slave, and she would receive visits from the master at his pleasure. She would be his concubine. She was only fifteen years old at the time. James Norcom was fifty. She later described how she "had rather live and die in jail, than drag on, from day to day, through such a living death." She knew she would *never* move into the cottage (*ILSG*, 69–70, 34, 359).

But what could she do? She became anxious and distressed. "I was determined," she said, "that the master, whom I so hated and loathed, who had blighted the prospects of my youth, and made my life a desert, should not, after my long struggle with him, succeed at last in trampling his victim under his feet." The wheels in her head began turning. She had an idea. It was something she would never have done under different circumstances. She knew it was immoral, and it broke her heart. But she also knew it was clever enough that it just might work to defeat Norcom and win her the precious freedom she so desired. "I knew what I did," she explained, "and I did it with deliberate calculation. . . . I became desperate, and made a plunge into the abyss" (*ILSG*, 69).

Living next door to Grandma Molly was a wealthy, young, unmarried, white lawyer named Samuel Sawyer. Sawyer had always been a friend to Molly and Harriet and had shown genuine concern for Harriet's well-being, knowing something of the hell Norcom was putting her through. Harriet took advantage of the opportunity. She would now execute her plan against Norcom.

Harriet allowed her friendship with Sawyer to develop into something more. "By degrees," she said, "a more tender feeling crept into my heart. . . . There is something akin to freedom," Harriet continued, "in having a lover who has no control over you, except that which he gains by kindness and attachment." Her plan, of course, was more calculated than just a love affair. She explained: "I knew nothing would enrage [Dr. Norcom] so much as to know that I favored another; and it was something to triumph over my tyrant even in that small way. I thought he would revenge himself by selling me, and I was sure my friend, [Mr. Sawyer], would buy me" (*ILSG*, 70–71).

In order to make herself even more repulsive to Norcom, thus hopefully compelling him to sell her rapidly, Harriet allowed herself to become pregnant with Sawyer's child.

The day finally came when Norcom's cottage was built. He came to Harriet to transport her to her new home. She stood before him boldly and declared: "I will never go there. In a few months I shall be a mother." Norcom was speechless. Dumbfounded. All he could do was stand up and exit the room without a word (*ILSG*, 72).

IN HARRIET'S WORDS

"But, O, ye happy women, whose purity has been sheltered from childhood, who have been free to choose the objects of your affection, whose homes are protected by law, do not judge the poor desolate slave girl too severely! If slavery had been abolished, I, also, could have married the man of my choice . . . but I was struggling alone in the powerful grasp of the demon Slavery. . . . I felt as if I was forsaken by God and man" (*ILSG*, 69-70).

Sawyer promised Harriet and Grandma Molly that he would care for the baby and that he would make every possible effort to purchase Harriet and the child from Norcom. Norcom refused any offer to sell Harriet and instead sought to exact revenge. Unfortunately for him, his wife believed that Harriet's child belonged to her own husband and thus forbade Harriet from living in their home (*ILSG*, 98). In that respect, Harriet's plan was working perfectly. Norcom of course knew the child was not his, but he couldn't convince his wife of that fact. Days after Harriet had told him she was pregnant, he returned to her and confronted her.

"I command you," he said, " . . . tell me whether the father of your child is white or black." Harriet told him the truth. He sprang upon her like a wild animal, grabbing her arm in a way to make her believe he might break it.

"Do you love him?" he sneered.

"I am thankful that I don't despise him," Harriet replied.

He raised his hand to strike her, but then put it back down. "I don't know what it is that keeps me from killing you," he threatened.

He then commanded her to move into the cottage and never see Sawyer again. Harriet refused the proposition, knowing Norcom had only so many options now. With his jealous wife stalking him, with Grandma Molly pointing fingers at him, with the townsfolk of Edenton gossiping about his evil ways with his slaves, and now with a prominent young attorney at Harriet's side, Norcom was losing his grip. He was stuck. Harriet had boxed him in.

Harriet would move in permanently with Grandma Molly to have her baby. Sawyer would visit and care for her. Norcom would also visit, always reminding Harriet that she was *his* slave, that he would *never* sell her, and that her baby, once born, would make a fine addition to his stock of human chattel. Neither Harriet nor Molly could stop him from coming, as Harriet was still his property by law. Though they knew Harriet had won the

GRANDMA MOLLY: A POWERFUL ALLY

The town of Edenton, for the most part, respected and appreciated Molly Horniblow, known lovingly to them as "Aunt Molly." One day, in her own home, Molly walked in on Norcom beating her Harriet with blow after blow. Molly would have none of that. She was a free woman whose influence among the people made her a force to be reckoned with. "Get out of my house," she screamed at the old man. "Do you know who you are talking to?" he shot back. "Yes, I know very well who I am talking to." The cowardly Norcom left the house in rage, but not before hearing this declaration from Molly: "Go home, and take care of your wife and children, and you will have enough to do, without watching my family." Then the stinging, prophetic warning: "I tell you what, [Dr. Norcom]," she blasted, "you ain't got many more years to live, and you'd better be saying your prayers. It will take 'em all, and more too, to wash the dirt off your soul" (*ILSG*, 106).

battle, Norcom was always there to remind them that the war was far from over.

Eventually a baby boy was born. Harriet named him Joseph. As much as she instantly loved the baby, she found herself having mixed feelings. "I loved to watch his infant slumbers," she wrote, "but always there was a dark cloud over my enjoyment. I could never forget that he was a slave. Sometimes I wished that he might die in his infancy. . . . Death is better than slavery" (*ILSG*, 80).

Within a few years, nineteen-year-old Harriet became pregnant with a second baby by Sam Sawyer. When Norcom learned of the second pregnancy, he stormed into Molly's home with a

THE NAT TURNER INSURRECTION

In 1831, while Harriet Jacobs was figuring out the best way forward in her tumultuous life in Edenton, a historic event occurred in neighboring Virginia. The slave Nat Turner had decided he was done. With a small group of rebels, he went from plantation to plantation, killing slave owners, stealing guns and horses, and recruiting other slaves in his revolt against slavery. He was eventually caught and executed. But the effect of the insurrection had brutal consequences for slaves everywhere, including those in Edenton. The white population felt a strong show of brutal force was required to deter any thoughts of future insurrection. The white militias arose in and around Edenton and began their raids. Evidence was planted in the homes of innocent black families so the militias could have an excuse to make an example of them and scare all the others. Harriet was witness to black "men, women and children [being] whipped till blood stood in puddles at their feet" (*ILSG*, 68).

Harriet knew the militias would be coming to Grandma Molly's home. Harriet also knew that most of the militias were made up of poor-white country folk who loved taking their frustrations out on slaves, as it was the only way that they, in their pitiful state, could feel superior to something. Harriet knew that she and Grandma Molly, though by no means wealthy, were still better off than most of those militiamen, so she fixed and decorated their home especially nicely to welcome the raiders with the shocking news that they lived worse than this black Edenton family. Harriet also knew that she and Grandma Molly were so well liked by their prominent white neighbors that they would ultimately be protected.

The plan worked. When the cowardly intruders entered the home, they didn't know how to respond. They saw things they did not possess. They also discovered that Harriet could read and write—something many of them could not do. "Look here, mammy," one of the white militiamen muttered to Grandma Molly, "you seem to feel mighty gran' 'cause you got all them 'ere fixens. White folks oughter have 'em all." Harriet called in a white neighbor, who happily took his position in the house, making the rabble in arms nervous. Harriet boldly walked up to the men and took her and Molly's possessions out of their thieving hands. As they had found no evidence of rebellion in the home, it was now time for them to leave, and they began to make their embarrassed exit.

But before leaving, another soldier asked aloud, "Where'd the damned niggers git all dis sheet an' table clarf." Grandma Molly turned defiantly to the white man, and declared confidently, "You may be sure we didn't pilfer 'em from your houses" (*ILSG*, 81–84).

pair of scissors in his hand. He jumped upon poor Harriet and cut all of her hair off as punishment, while simultaneously striking her (*ILSG*, 99).

Notwithstanding the constant abuse, the baby came, a little girl. Harriet named her Louisa, but called her Lulu. The same bittersweet feeling ensued. "Slavery is terrible for men;" she wrote, "but it is far more terrible for women. Superadded to the burden common to all, *they* have wrongs, and sufferings, and mortifications peculiarly their own" (*ILSG*, 100).

Harriet tried her best to be a good mother. She wanted her children to be baptized, but Norcom prohibited it. The wicked master himself had been baptized in his adulthood and had eventually become a warden at St. Paul's Episcopal Church. The everdefiant and spunky Harriet had confronted him one day regarding the hypocrisy of it all. After Norcom had tried to seduce her once again, Harriet reminded him that he was now a churchman and shouldn't talk like that. He then lectured her on morality, telling her that if she were to become his concubine, "if you are faithful to me, you will be as virtuous as my wife." Harriet rebuked him, telling him that his own Bible contradicted such ideas. "How dare you preach to me about your infernal Bible!" he screamed at the young girl, his voice "hoarse with rage." He continued: "What right have you, who are my negro, to talk to me about what you would like, and what you wouldn't like? I am your master" (*ILSG*, 96–97).

Notwithstanding such hypocrisy among men, Harriet loved God. And so, when Master Norcom left town, Molly and Harriet quickly and quietly ushered the two children into the church and had them secretly baptized (*ILSG*, 101).

Harriet loved being a mother to her precious children and knew she would do anything to provide for their happiness and well-being. But Norcom would not leave them alone. He often threatened Harriet as she tended to her children, saying with a wicked smile, "These brats will bring me a handsome sum of money one of these days." No words could be more terrifying to a mother, especially from a man who had the power to make good on the threat.

The children, as children are often equipped to do, sensed the darkness when Norcom would enter their otherwise happy home. Harriet remembered that baby Lulu would "shut her eyes and hide her face on my shoulder whenever she saw him; and [Joseph], still a child no older than 5, would inquire, 'What makes that bad man come here so many times? Does he want to hurt us?'"

Sam Sawyer hated seeing Harriet and her children suffer so. He went again to Norcom and pled with him to sell the family over to his care. Norcom refused immediately. As much as he was in love with money, he was more in love with power. Norcom then followed the offer up with yet another visit to Grandma Molly's home.

Master Norcom sat down across from Harriet and looked at her with spite and disgust. "You are mine;" he declared, his putrid words striking the heart of Harriet, "and you shall be mine for life. There lives no human being that can take you out of slavery."

Then, as was his habit, he violently grabbed Harriet's arm and launched into a tirade of threats and accusations against her. Little Joseph was in the room and began to scream in terror. Harriet told her boy to run to Grandma, who was in another room. But Joseph was too much like his mother. He wouldn't run from the attacking darkness. Instead, he would engage it. The five-year-old child ran to Harriet and threw his little arms around her body to protect his mommy.

A CLUE IN THE OLD CHURCH RECORDS

Hidden in the old membership records of St. Paul's Episcopal Church is possible evidence of the resilience and faith of young Harriet. In the records is a note about one "Hariet J. Norcom." (Slave owners often forced their own last names onto their slaves, like branding on cattle.) Among other membership notes documented under the year 1832 (the year before Lulu was born), the record states that Harriet "ceased to commune."

The current rector of the church, Reverend J. Gilliam, has noted how odd the note about Harriet is. A similar note is nowhere to be found in any of the other church records. A logical conclusion is that James Norcom put the note in the records to make sure Harriet was kept out of the church community, perhaps fearful that she would reveal the true character of the "churchman."

But more important, this discovery reveals the true character of Harriet. She would not let the evil ways of men keep her children from God. And so, this "excommunicated" slave girl would defy the wicked systems of the world and smuggle her children into the church (presumably finding some compliant church officer) in order to make peace—not with the church that had ousted her, but between herself, her children, and their Father in Heaven.[11]

Mrs Hariet I Norcom ceased to Commune

This act of defiance was too much for the master, who then picked up the helpless boy and threw him across the room, knocking him unconscious. Harriet immediately moved toward her suffering child while Norcom made every effort to restrain her. She broke free from the serpent, then threw herself over the seemingly lifeless little body.

Harriet described what happened next. "I picked up my insensible child, and when I turned my tormentor was gone. Anxiously I bent over the little form, so pale and still; and when the brown eyes at last opened, I don't know whether I was very happy" (*ILSG*, 104–5).

Harriet made a promise to herself: "God being my helper," so began her covenant and proclamation, "[my children] should never pass into his hands. . . . I would rather see them killed than have them given up to his power" (*ILSG*, 103).

CHAPTER 4

NEW YORK CITY, CIRCA 2011

Not long ago, my small team of operators and I entered a tiny rented room inside a small, broken-down home in a poor, crime-ridden section of New York City.[12] In the room was a mattress stuffed into a corner. Lying on the mattress was a makeshift pillow that had been fashioned out of a sweatshirt and a piece of cloth, all tied together. Besides that, there were few material items in this room that had any value. But there was a person there who had as much value as any being on the planet. She was the sole inhabitant of the room, and had been for years. Her name was Mariana, and her story had brought me to tears—and had brought me and my operators to her room that day.

Around 2011, when Mariana was thirteen years old, she was kidnapped from her village in Guatemala. After fleeing an abusive home life, she had done her best to take care of herself, selling snow cones on the street. One day, a seemingly kind young man befriended her and offered her a job working in another city to the north. She took the job and left her village.

The young man then had her in his grips. Before she knew it, she was walking with him through the deserts of Mexico, then crossing illegally into the United States, walking days over mountains and sand, sleeping on rocks, shivering in the cold, until eventually coming to a highway. There she was picked up by a van and taken to New York City. What followed were five years of hell. She was kept in captivity in a small home with bars over all the windows. Her food was passed to her through these bars.

Worst of all, she had been coerced into a life of sex slavery. Like thousands of foreign children every year, she was smuggled into the United States and forced into the commercial sex trade. She was raped by up to forty or fifty men a day. Each session lasted about fifteen minutes, and she was made to perform whatever sex act the purchaser had ordered. Men working in conjunction with her slave owner had her daily itinerary well organized, driving her from house to house and bar to bar, making sure she didn't stay longer than fifteen minutes at each session. If she did, she would be punished severely.

By the time she was nearing adulthood, her childhood robbed clean, she saw a woman on TV telling her story of sex slavery—how she too had been kidnapped, how she had escaped, and how she was now a professional, prominent in her chosen field. Mariana took courage. She walked up to the man who controlled her and said defiantly: "I will be on TV one day. I will tell the world what you did to me! Others will escape because of it. And you will go to jail!" Her defiance was met with brutality and laughter.

But guess what? Within months of her protest, she did it! She escaped. She worked with police to have the man arrested and prosecuted, then reached out to me and told me of her plans: "Now that I'm free," she said, "I will be that girl I saw on TV. I will take down more bad guys. I will rescue more victims."

We responded to her call, went to her home, verified her story, took her out of the squalor she lived in, and signed her up to fulfill her dreams. She is now in a different city, safely healing. And she is plotting; she is turning the table on the evil that haunted her through so much of her life. Hundreds, maybe thousands, will find their way out of darkness because of her light.

Never have I seen a modern story that so closely parallels the life of Harriet Jacobs. And never have I seen anyone come so close to matching the courage of Jacobs.

In the meantime, my team seeks ways to find the millions of other "Marianas" that exist in the world. And we hope—we dream and scheme—that we might rescue them from their captors before they enter the darkest hell that Mariana was forced to endure. Such was our hope and plan with Gardy, with Mia, and with Marky. These kids had been taken and placed on the path into a nightmare that gets worse and worse as each day passes. Could we get there in time? Could we get them before the fullness of evil attacked and enveloped them?

As it turned out, the link to all three kids—the bridge that might cut the darkness off at the pass—was Gardy's father, Guesno Mardy. You'll recall from earlier that, after reading about him in a news article, I called Guesno. I then flew him to the United States from Haiti. We met for dinner at a quiet restaurant. And this is what happened.

My first reaction when I saw the Haitian father was one of surprise. To me, he looked way too happy—in both his eyes and his smile—to have lost a child. And it was a pure happiness, a light. I would eventually figure out what that light was and how he got it; when I did, it would change my whole perspective on life. But for now I was more concerned about Gardy than I was about Guesno. I wanted to help find the child.

I explained to Guesno that I was a special agent and a certified undercover operator for the United States government, that I had seen the news article about his son, and that I wanted to help.

Guesno was beyond grateful. In his thick Haitian Creole accent, he began recounting the story of how his son had been taken. He explained that he had fired an employee named Carlos

Guesno Mardy

for embezzling money from the orphanage that Guesno and his wife, Marjorie, had started many years earlier to help the thousands of abandoned children in their country. Carlos was a member of the Christian church congregation that Guesno led in downtown Port-au-Prince. Guesno, always forgiving, had encouraged Carlos to keep coming to church, even though he could no longer work for Guesno's orphanage.

Carlos, however, used Guesno's forgiving heart against him. Carlos wanted revenge. So he teamed up with some trafficking thugs and hatched a plan. Carlos would kidnap Gardy and give him to the thugs; then together they would ransom the child back to the Mardy family. Carlos would play the innocent churchgoer during the scheme, carrying out his role as the eyes and ears of his criminal partners, always there to encourage Guesno to make the payment and get his son back. Carlos would make up his lost income, the thugs would make something as well, and Guesno would have his son back in short order. No real harm done to anyone.

On Sunday, December 6, 2009, Carlos lurked in the back of the church, waiting for his opportunity to roll out his plan.

Guesno didn't know me well enough at our first meeting to tell me this, but later he would. It is his most painful memory.

"Tim," Guesno would later confess to me, after we had become dear friends, "Gardy knew something was going to happen to him that day. He just knew."

It was one of the few times Guesno ever broke down in my presence. I put my arm around him as he continued.

"He usually loved going to the children's Sunday School class. But this time, he would not go. He would not leave me. I had to teach classes and administer meetings, and he just hung on to my neck, holding me as tightly as possible. I just taught my classes all day, using one arm to hold him as he snuggled his little face into my neck. I even held him as I conducted the final worship service in the chapel."

I could hardly breathe as I listened.

"Then," Guesno said, barely getting the words out, "when the final church service ended, I forced him off my body and insisted that he walk the short distance down the steps from the podium platform where we were and into the congregation, where his mother and four siblings would receive him. I had people to talk to and my arms were tired. He obeyed me. He was a very, very obedient child."

The tears were now flowing fast, and I held Guesno tighter with my arm around his shoulder.

"I never saw him again after that." Guesno barely squeaked this last sentence out as his throat tightened and convulsed.

As we sat in the restaurant at this first meeting, Guesno explained how it was in this moment that Carlos saw his opportunity and struck. He intercepted the child and walked him calmly out to the parking lot of the church. Gardy knew Carlos. He trusted him enough to go with him. A thug on a motorcycle was

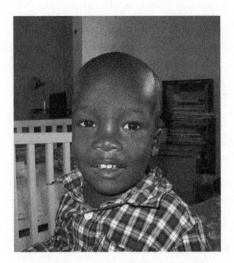

Gardy Mardy, almost three years old,
just weeks before he was kidnapped

waiting on the street outside. Carlos placed Gardy on the motor-cycle and, just like that, Gardy was gone.

Shortly after Guesno and Marjorie realized their boy was nowhere to be found, the ransom call came in. The thugs used Carlos's phone to make the call. They used his phone on purpose; they were now scheming not only against the Mardy family but against Carlos as well. Guesno immediately raised the several thou-sand dollars required to pay the ransom, and it was delivered to the criminals. But Gardy was not returned. Why give the boy back when he could be sold for additional money into the black market?

And since it was Carlos's phone that was used, and since Carlos had every motive, the thugs knew he was their perfect fall guy. Carlos—while definitely a bad guy in this, needing to go to jail—would not have approved of a permanent kidnapping, so the thugs needed to get rid of him. Plus, they wouldn't have to share their take with him if he was locked up. Also, by setting up an arrest in a poorly functioning judicial system in a country where kids are being kidnapped weekly with little to no response by the police, they could make it look like progress had been made in the case. The police could then justify not putting as much attention on the Gardy case, which might give the thugs a little more wiggle room and cause the authorities to focus their limited resources elsewhere. This trafficking ring had thought this out; they knew what they were doing.

Haitian authorities arrested Carlos almost immediately. But to this day, though Carlos is still sitting in a jail cell, he has refused to provide much information. He knows that if he confesses too much, he will never get out.

By the time Guesno finished telling his story, neither of us had touched the food that had been served. We had no appetite.

"Guesno," I asked, "what is being done to find your son now?"

Guesno answered my question with a strange question that seemed totally out of context. "Do you have children, Tim?"

"Yes," I responded, my eyes matching the intensity I was reading in his.

"Then let me ask you something. . . ." He hesitated. He must have known the question was somewhat cruel. But he went forward with it anyway. "Could you get in bed and sleep at night, knowing that one of your children's beds was empty?"

I knew the answer was no, but I couldn't get the word out, as instant tears and emotion blocked my ability to vocalize. I just shook my head.

"I don't sleep, Tim. I haven't slept since they took my Gardy."

I grabbed his hand as tears flowed freely between us.

He finally gained his composure. He then continued: "Since I don't sleep, I walk the streets of Port-au-Prince every night. I arbitrarily pick some neighborhood. The darker the better. The more dangerous the better. I walk. And I pray. I plead with heaven that I will hear Gardy cry out for me."

Minutes passed in silence. I still could not speak. I couldn't find words. So we sat at the table saying nothing.

I finally broke the silence: "Guesno, are there any leads at all?"

"Yes," he responded, "phone records and a few vague statements made by Carlos led us to believe that Gardy was or is being kept in an orphanage in downtown Port-au-Prince."

"Did the police raid the place?" I asked.

"No. It doesn't work that way in Haiti. They need more evidence. They don't believe they have enough to go in."

"So, you get more evidence!" I almost shouted. "You go undercover. You engage the evil players! If they are selling kids, you put yourself in a position to buy one! You record the evidence. You make arrests. You rescue children!"

I was out of breath and quite amped up.

"We have tried to get into the place," Guesno responded. "I even rented a room next door and sat on the roof with binoculars, trying to see in over the large cement walls. I couldn't see anything. They don't let anyone in."

Guesno sensed my frustration.

"Tim, you can't get in. Nobody can."

I then leaned over the table and said something to Guesno that would generally be ill-advised for a professional to say in a situation like this—and it was something that would later haunt me, throwing me into deep anxiety for having said it. But I don't regret it, because I meant it.

"I *promise* you, Guesno," I said, looking him squarely in the eye, "I *will* get into that place, and then I'll never stop until we find your son. I give you my word."

The smile came back immediately. He thanked me. More important, he believed me.

In the weeks that followed, I worked every angle to make the

Gardy investigation a United States government case. The problem: It just was not. It was a Haitian crime under Haitian jurisdiction. There was little I could do. Had I been my own boss, I would have had to tell myself the same thing. We had no legal or jurisdictional authority to act. I thought about working the Gardy case in my spare time, but I didn't have enough personal leave time or money to do the case any justice. I was stuck.

But I had made a promise. And, as I said, Guesno believed me.

Deep anxiety set in. The stress was born not only of the promise I had made, which I now didn't know how to keep, but from everything I had learned in my career over the previous decade. Within months of becoming a special agent for Homeland Security, I was asked to drop everything and help start a Child Crimes Unit. That led to joining the Internet Crimes Against Children Task Force and later being trained as an undercover operator to infiltrate criminal organizations responsible for kidnapping, trafficking, and exploiting children. I had traveled around the United States and foreign countries posing as a sex tourist, a purveyor of child sex, a pedophile, and whatever else I needed to in order to do my job. The deeper I got into it, the more heartbreaking it became. The statistics—the number of children estimated to be stuck in this darkness—continued to grow at astonishing rates. And somehow, in this moment, Gardy represented all of them; he represented all the lost children I could never before access.

It was like I knew too much. I knew the problem was real. I knew how to investigate the Gardy case. I believed we could rescue him and the other kids in that false orphanage. I began thinking about the millions of others outside my jurisdiction. I'm ashamed to say that I wished, in that moment, that I had not learned these things. Life was better when I did not know. I also wished I had a better excuse so that I could go back to Guesno and tell him there was nothing I could do. I didn't feel like I could do that because I knew there *was* one option, but I was too cowardly to even mention it out loud. Hence the guilt—and the anxiety.

As the reality of my situation became clearer and clearer, I found myself sitting alone one night in my living room, head thrust deeply into my hands. In that moment, I felt the only thing that could possibly ease any of my pain. I felt the warm, gentle hands of my wife, Katherine, on my shoulders.

"What am I going to do?" I asked, fighting back tears.

She smiled. "I know exactly what you are going to do. You are going to find that little boy."

Turning to her, I said almost desperately, "But the *only* way to do that would be to quit my job and somehow raise money on my own to fund the rescue. That's insane. We have six kids!"

"That's right," she said. "But we will do it anyway."

My anxiety increased. I was way too weak to do such a risky thing. I would be going from the most secure job on the planet—federal employee—to the most insecure job on the planet—founder of a nonprofit organization.

"There's no way I'm doing that," I told Katherine. "Did I mention we have six children and they all eat food? And food actually costs money?"

She stayed calm through my sarcasm, and I was too frazzled and emotional to even attempt a fake laugh at my own stupid joke.

"Gardy is a real child," she said. "His family's suffering is real. The other lost children outside of your jurisdiction are real too. God knows them and loves them. And you know how to get them."

I allowed some peace to enter my soul as she spoke.

"You don't think that once you act, heaven will open the doors?" she asked, almost rhetorically.

I knew the answer to her question was *yes,* although I couldn't say I fully believed it yet. But Katherine knew. And I knew that she knew, and that would be enough for now.

It wasn't long before I was turning in my badge and gun. I recruited a team of former law enforcement, CIA, and Navy SEAL operators. And we raised enough money to go in search of Gardy.

Today, the foundation that we started has only grown and grown. We are currently at work in more than a dozen different countries, including the United States. Always working with and under the legal authority of local law enforcement (this is not a vigilante program), we have rescued many hundreds of children and have protected, cared for, and helped heal thousands.

As a private, nonprofit organization, we can also do something I was not really able to do before. We can include private citizens in our efforts and use their collective power for good to end the trafficking of children. No great societal plague was ever eradicated without the help of the citizenry. This problem needs a grassroots movement, where the masses can rise up and join hands with the governments of the world, and together we can find success. So far, it's working.

The point is, Katherine was right from the beginning. She had shown immense courage. She had been a light in the darkness. Guesno had also been a light. And many others as well. This light was so important to me, especially in the beginning of our rescue efforts, that I searched for it everywhere I could. When I had to pick a name for the foundation, the name, of course, had to reflect that light. As I explained in the introduction, the name came quickly: *Operation Underground Railroad.*

And of all those great rescuers from the nineteenth century, none impressed me or inspired me more than Harriet Jacobs. Her sacrifice. Her bravery. Her spirit. Her light. If only we could all be like her, how different the world would be today.

A SAMPLING OF
O.U.R. OPERATIONS WORLDWIDE

OPERATION TRIPLE TAKE*

123 SURVIVORS **RESCUED**

20 TRAFFICKERS **ARRESTED**

*3 MISSIONS

COLOMBIA 2014 OUR
OPERATION UNDERGROUND RAILROAD

OPERATION MUNDO NUEVO II

29 SURVIVORS **RESCUED**

7 TRAFFICKERS **ARRESTED**

DOMINICAN REPUBLIC 2015 OUR
OPERATION UNDERGROUND RAILROAD

OPERATION WHALE WATCH

24 SURVIVORS **RESCUED**

5 TRAFFICKERS **ARRESTED**

MEXICO 2016 OUR
OPERATION UNDERGROUND RAILROAD

OPERATION HAPPY KHLOY

6 SURVIVORS **RESCUED**

1 TRAFFICKERS **ARRESTED**

CAMBODIA 2017 OUR
OPERATION UNDERGROUND RAILROAD

OPERATION NET NANNY 11

7 SURVIVORS **RESCUED**

10 TRAFFICKERS **ARRESTED**

USA 2018 OUR
OPERATION UNDERGROUND RAILROAD

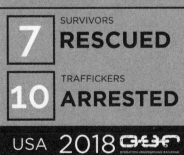

OPERATION RUBY

56 SURVIVORS **RESCUED**

2 TRAFFICKERS **ARRESTED**

INDIA 2018 OUR
OPERATION UNDERGROUND RAILROAD

CHAPTER 5

EDENTON, NORTH CAROLINA, 1835

I saw a mother lead seven children to the auction-block," wrote Harriet Jacobs. "She knew that some of them would be taken from her; but they took all. . . . Before night her children were all far away. She begged the trader to tell her where he intended to take them; this he refused to do. . . . I met that mother in the street, and her wild, haggard face still lives to-day in my mind. She wrung her hands in anguish, and exclaimed, 'Gone! All gone! Why don't God kill me?' I had no words wherewith to comfort her. Instances of this kind are of daily, yea, of hourly occurrence" (ILSG, 19).

On another occasion, Harriet witnessed a similar scene. While she was worshipping one Sunday in an all-black church, she looked on in extreme sadness as a slave woman stood and sobbed uncontrollably. Between fits of tears and rage, she explained to the congregation how each and every one of her children had been sold out from under her. The slave mother further explained that her last child, a young girl, the only one who had remained with her, was finally sold just days earlier. She struck her chest and declared: "I can't tell you what is in here! They've got all my children. Last week they took the last one. God only knows where they've sold her . . . O! O! Pray for her brothers and sisters! I've got nothing to live for now. God make my time short!"

As she sat down, Harriet noted that she "quiver[ed] in every limb." The congregation then sang a hymn that was popular with slaves: "Ole Satan's church is here below, / Up to God's free church I hope to go" (*ILSG*, 91–92).

This was the reality of Harriet's Edenton, the reality of black America. And the writing was on the wall: Harriet knew that if she did not act, her children could easily, even probably, meet a similar fate. She was not going to wait around for that to happen; she would do anything to keep the promise she made to her children. One way or another, she would get them to freedom.

One-third of slave marriages ended when the master sold the man or the woman. Over one-half of all slave children lost at least one of their parents (and many times both of their parents) for the same reason.[13]

One day, as this young mother was tending to her precious Joseph and her beautiful little Lulu, always planning and scheming their route to freedom, Master Norcom came knocking. He had come with a dangerous proposition, one that would force Harriet's hand and compel her into a daring liberation scheme.

"I have seen very little of you of late," he said calmly, "but my interest in you is unchanged."

Few words could have possibly felt as threatening to Harriet's soul.

Norcom continued, "If you agree to what I am about to propose, you and [your children] shall be free."

Harriet smelled a trap.

Norcom defined the proposal—the conditions of this "freedom." "There must be no communication of any kind between you and [your children's] father," he explained. "I will procure a cottage, where you and the children can live together. Your labor shall be light, such as sewing for my family."

Norcom waited for an answer. Harriet knew that if she accepted, she was agreeing to be his concubine. And Lulu would be next. Harriet remained silent.

"Why don't you speak?" Norcom asked. "What more do you wait for?"

"Nothing, sir," was the reply.

"Then you accept my offer?"

"No, sir," Harriet said decisively.

Norcom's anger was immediate. But instead of striking her, he added texture to the proposition. His son, James Norcom Jr., lived and worked on the Norcom plantation several miles outside of Edenton. The doctor would leverage that possession to try to compel Harriet into compliance.

"You must either accept my offer, or you and your children shall be sent to your young master's plantation . . . and your children shall fare like the rest of the negro children. I give you one week to consider it."

"[I'm] ready to give my answer now," the girl shot back, ever defiant.

"I will not receive it now," said Norcom. With that, he left Harriet alone to consider her options.

He came back a week later and asked Harriet what she had decided.

"I am ready to go to the plantation," Harriet told him, much to his shock.

Rejected once again by the girl he just couldn't get his hands around, Norcom went into a fit of rage.

"Very well," he sneered, "go to the plantation, and my curse go with you. Your boy shall be put to work, and he shall soon be sold; and your girl shall be raised for the purpose of selling well. Go your own ways!" With those fiery words, he stormed out of the house.

Perhaps Harriet's decision seemed rash. Prideful. Irrational. Indeed, on the surface it appeared as though she had only precipitated the very thing she feared the most. But Harriet's intentions and goals with all her decisions, especially with this one, did not float around on the surface. Her thoughts were deep, her planning complex, her cunning superior—much more so than those of the white, educated doctor of Edenton.

She later said of this fateful decision: "I was resolved that I would foil my master and save my children, or I would perish in the attempt" (*ILSG*, 107–9).

Harriet left for the plantation. As per her plan, once she arrived she became the hardest-working slave there. She went above and beyond in all her duties. She was polite and respectful. She made herself almost indispensable to the James Norcom Jr. family. They began to trust her, even to like her. They grew soft toward her—and that was exactly where she needed them. She knew that was when they would begin taking their watchful eyes off her. And that was when she would strike against the demon called slavery. "I had a woman's pride, and a mother's love for my children;" Harriet later wrote of her feelings concerning this time in her life, "and I resolved that out of the darkness of this hour a brighter dawn should rise for them. My master had power and law on his side; I had a determined will. There is might in each" (*ILSG*, 110).

The game was on.

◆ ◆ ◆

Harriet made the trip from the plantation back into Edenton whenever she could, sometimes sneaking back without permission of the master. She couldn't stand to be kept apart from her children, who at least for now had been permitted to remain with Grandma Molly. Once, upon her return, when little Joseph saw her he excitedly asked, "O mother! you ain't dead, are you? They didn't cut off your head at the plantation, did they?" (*ILSG*, 113).

Harriet didn't know exactly when she would take her flight, and thus execute one of the most daring and harrowing slave escapes of all time. But it seems that, during one of these visits to Edenton, she sensed the timing was close. Very close.

It was a Sunday. Harriet went to pay a Sabbath visit to perhaps the most sacred spot in Edenton, then or now. It was a slave cemetery, the very place her mother and father were buried. It was sacred to her because death itself was sacred to her. "There the wicked cease from troubling," Harriet wrote, "and there the weary be at rest. There the prisoners rest together; they hear not the voice of the oppressor; the servant is free from his master" (*ILSG*, 116).

As Harriet entered the cemetery, known as Providence, she passed by the site of the old slave church, which had been torn down by the masters and left in ruins as "punishment" (or as a scare tactic) in the wake of the Nat Turner rebellion. As she passed the ruined church, she seemed to hear her father's voice coming from the site, instructing her to tarry no more in slavery, but rather to fight until she "reached freedom or the grave" (*ILSG*, 117). Of course, Harriet had resolved long before that the freedom she desired was not so much for her as it was for her children, particularly for her little Lulu, whose fate in Edenton could be nothing but hell. You will recall Harriet's words: "Slavery is terrible for men; but it is far more terrible for women" (*ILSG*, 100).

These were her thoughts as she knelt down in the graveyard.

PROVIDENCE CEMETERY

The Providence cemetery was eventually lost due to overgrowth and abandonment. It was rediscovered in 2000 and rededicated in 2001.

"The graveyard was in the woods, and twilight was coming on. Nothing broke the death-like stillness except the occasional twitter of a bird. My spirit was overawed by the solemnity of the scene. For more than ten years I had frequented this spot, but never had it seemed to me so sacred as now. A black stump, at the head of my mother's grave, was all that remained of a tree my father had planted. His grave was marked by a small wooden board, bearing his name, the letters of which were nearly obliterated. I knelt down and kissed them, and poured forth a prayer to God for guidance and support in the perilous step I was about to take. . . . I rushed on with renovated hopes. My trust in God had been strengthened by that prayer among the graves" (*ILSG*, 116–17).

"I knew the doom that awaited my fair baby in slavery," Harriet later recalled, "and I determined to save her from it, or perish in the attempt. I went to make this vow at the graves of my poor parents, in the burying-ground of the slaves" (*ILSG*, 117).

Harriet's vow could not have come at a better time, for something was about to happen on the Norcom plantation that would require her to flee once and for all. Barely a week had passed since the vow in the cemetery when Mrs. Norcom came to the plantation to visit her daughter-in-law, the woman who had just married her son, James Jr., and was now mistress of the plantation and new mistress of Harriet. The jealous, hateful Mrs. Norcom had come to give orders to the new mistress. Harriet's children were to be snatched from the comfort of Grandma Molly's house and brought to the plantation to be "broke in." Harriet was the last to learn of the plan, and she learned of it accidentally. In fact, on the day she learned about it, she also learned that it was to happen the very next day; indeed, her children were to be trafficked into the plantation on the morrow. "It nerved me to direct action," explained Harriet (*ILSG*, 120–21).

Harriet's plan was a smart one. If she could escape and hide, then the Norcoms wouldn't dare bring Joseph and Lulu out to the plantation, for who would take care of two small children? As the children were not yet old enough to labor, they would only be a drain on the Norcom business. With Harriet gone, the children would be left at Grandma Molly's, which would buy Harriet time to implement phase two of her plan—a much trickier proposition—to get the children purchased away from Norcom and into the Northern states.

That night Harriet waited until everyone in the Norcom house was asleep. They weren't watching her, since they had been deceived into trusting her. When the lights went out that night at the plantation, Harriet simply opened a window and quietly slipped out. As her feet hit the cold ground outside, she noticed large drops of rain falling upon her head. She also noticed how dark that particular night was. She dropped onto her knees in the wet and muddy soil and pleaded to heaven for guidance. Then she jumped to her feet and disappeared into the unknown darkness (*ILSG*, 123).

Harriet hid in various places, including the thick woods that surrounded Edenton. One night while she was hiding in the woods, she was bitten. "Suddenly," recalled Harriet, "a reptile of some kind seized my leg. In my fright, I struck a blow which loosened its hold. . . . I could not see what it was; I only knew it was something cold and slimy. The pain I felt soon indicated that the bite was poisonous" (*ILSG*, 127). Harriet got word to her family that something must be done soon, as she could not survive long on the run.

Dr. Norcom was furious when he learned that Harriet had disappeared. He sent patrols out everywhere in search of her, but her hiding places were just too good. Grandma Molly's house was searched, top to bottom. When they got to Harriet's trunk, they noticed all her clothes were gone. This made Norcom believe she had fled town, most likely to the North. Norcom made sure every vessel leaving in that direction was searched as thoroughly as Molly's house had been.

The truth was, Harriet knew that a northern trek would have been next to impossible, with so many patrols on the lookout. She knew she would have to hide in town, at least until things cooled off. But she wanted to distract and mislead. She wanted Norcom to believe she had moved north so that the patrols would waste time and resources looking in the wrong place. So, on the very Sunday when she had made her graveyard vow, she had also

$100 REWARD

WILL be given for the apprehension and delivery of my Servant Girl HARRIET. She is a light mulatto, 21 years of age, about 5 feet 4 inches high, of a thick and corpulent habit, having on her head a thick covering of black hair that curls naturally, but which can be easily combed straight. She speaks easily and fluently, and has an agreeable carriage and address. Being a good seamstress, she has been accustomed to dress well, has a variety of very fine clothes, made in the prevailing fashion, and will probably appear, if abroad, tricked out in gay and fashionable finery. As this girl absconded from the plantation of my son without any known cause or provocation, it is probable she designs to transport herself to the North.

The above reward, with all reasonable charges, will be given for apprehending her, or securing her in any prison or jail within the U. States.

All persons are hereby forewarned against harboring or entertaining her, or being in any way instrumental in her escape, under the most rigorous penalties of the law.

JAMES NORCOM.

Edenton, N. C. June 30   tr&2w

Advertisement offering $100 reward for the capture of Harriet Jacobs

emptied her trunk of all her clothes and hidden them away with a friend. Her plan to make Norcom believe she had left town was working (*ILSG,* 117–18, 125).

Norcom's search was failing. So his wicked mind conjured up another idea. He took Joseph and Lulu and threw the six- and two-year-old children into the county jail. He also took Aunt Betty and Harriet's brother, John (Norcom owned both of them), and threw them into the jail as well. He did this to put pressure on Harriet to return for them. They were hostages. Bait. Though the children cried for their mother, Harriet knew that she needed to stay in hiding. As difficult as it was, she still believed her plan would free her children in the end (*ILSG*, 130).

During this intense period, Harriet had an unlikely friend rise to the occasion. Her name was Martha Blount. She was white, and she owned slaves. Her home sat at the corner of Queen and Broad Streets. Martha was about to do something that she knew could ruin her family forever and send her to prison. But she did it anyway because it was the right thing to do. She went to Molly and told her she wanted to help Harriet in her escape. Molly looked at the woman and wondered what to do. Was it a trap? Had Norcom sent her? But, as Molly looked into Martha's eyes, she noted they were honest eyes—eyes that seemed to be saying, "Trust me!" Molly told Martha where Harriet was.

"I will conceal her," Martha promised. They made a plan to get word to Harriet to meet at a certain place before being

Chowan County jail, where Harriet's children were taken

escorted into the Blount home. Martha said that nobody, even in her own home, could know of the scheme, with the exception of "Old Betty," Martha's slave and cook. "She is so faithful," declared Martha, "that I would trust my own life with her." Old Betty was perhaps the most optimistic, jovial human being in town, and she would be happy to risk everything, along with her mistress, to rescue Harriet. With the quick plan made, Martha readied herself to leave and get to work. She needed to instruct Old Betty and find excuses to send everyone else in her home out on errands so nobody would see Harriet enter. Before leaving, she turned to Molly.

"You must solemnly promise that my name shall never be mentioned," Martha warned. "If such a thing should become known, it would ruin me and my family."

Of course Molly would make and keep that promise. But she was too overwhelmed with emotion and gratitude to say so in the moment. She couldn't say anything. "She was unable to thank the lady for this noble deed; overcome by her emotions, she sank on her knees and sobbed like a child" (*ILSG*, 128).

Harriet was told to meet that night at a certain place. She was told nothing else—no names were given. She dutifully showed up at the rendezvous point and was surprised and relieved to see Old Betty waiting for her there. Old Betty had been her friend for years. They fled together into the pitch-black night, Harriet's leg still throbbing in pain from the reptile bite. Old Betty encouraged her on. They got to the house and made it in unseen by anyone.

"Honey, now you is safe," Old Betty declared. "Dem devils ain't coming to search *dis* house. When I get you into missis' safe place, I will bring some nice hot supper." Old Betty walked

Harriet up to Martha's own room, where there was a closet room attached, perfect for hiding. Martha met them there.

"You will be safe here," Martha told Harriet kindly. "I keep this room to store away things that are out of use. The [slave] girls are not accustomed to be sent to it. . . . I always keep it locked, and Betty shall take care of the key. But you must be very careful, for my sake as well as your own; and you must never tell my secret; for it would ruin me and my family."

Harriet was speechless. Like Molly, she was overcome with gratitude.

"Keep up your courage," Martha told her. "I hope this state of things will not last long."

Harriet still could not speak. She later recalled: "How my heart overflowed with gratitude! Words choked in my throat; but I could have kissed the feet of my benefactress. For that deed of Christian womanhood, may God forever bless her!" Once secure in her place of refuge, Harriet kneeled once again. "I thanked the heavenly Father for this safe retreat," she recorded (*ILSG*, 129).

After about one month, with no sign of Harriet anywhere, Norcom decided to release Aunt Betty (not to be confused with Martha Blount's "Old Betty") from jail. Mrs. Norcom was tired of being her own housekeeper. As Harriet would mockingly explain later, "It was quite too fatiguing to order her dinner and eat it too." But Joseph, Lulu, and John were to remain locked up. Harriet's heart continued to ache for them.

She sent Old Betty to see her children from time to time. John would hold the kids up to the grated window, and the old lady would speak to them, then report back to Harriet. Old Betty would rehearse to Harriet how her babies spoke of their love for their mother and how badly they just wanted to see her. The tears would flow from Harriet's eyes as she heard the reports.

"Lors, chile!" Old Betty would exclaim, "what's you crying 'bout? . . . Don't be so chick'n hearted! If you does, you vil nebber git thro' dis world."

Harriet knew Old Betty was just trying to cheer her up. But Old Betty had never had any children. "She had never had little ones to clasp their arms round her neck;" Harriet later wrote, "she had never seen their soft eyes looking into hers; no sweet little voices had called her mother; she had never pressed her own infants to her heart, with that feeling that even in fetters there was something to live for. How could she realize my feelings?" (*ILSG*, 130–31).

While in jail, two-year-old Lulu came down with the measles. When Norcom found out, he brought her to his own home until she recovered. But when she entered the dark residence, she screamed and cried to be carried back into the jail. For she was loved there, and could not be fooled by the façade that was the Norcom home. As Harriet quipped, "The instincts of childhood are true."

Mrs. Norcom couldn't handle the crying, so she sent for one of her slaves to lock the child back up in the jail. "I can't stand her noise," Mrs. Norcom declared. "If she would be quiet I should like to keep the little minx. She would make a handy waiting-maid for my daughter by and by." As the child was hauled out of the house and sent back to jail, Mrs. Norcom blurted out this warning: "I hope the doctor will sell them as far as wind and water can carry them. As for their mother, her ladyship will find out yet what she gets by running away. She hasn't so much feeling for her children as a cow for its calf. If she had, she would have come back long ago, to get them out of jail . . . the good for nothing hussy! When she is caught, she shall stay in jail, in irons, for . . .

six months, and then be sold to a sugar plantation. I shall see her broke in yet" (*ILSG*, 131).

Norcom's plan was failing. His efforts to imprison and hold hostage two babies didn't have the effect he desired. Harriet was still nowhere to be found. He became desperate, employing everything he had in the search.

It seemed his efforts were about to pay off. In the middle of the night, hours after Lulu was taken back to prison, Norcom was walking by Molly's home and noticed a light on. He knocked at the door and Molly answered.

"I saw your light," declared the arrogant doctor, "and I thought I would just stop and tell you that I have found out where [Harriet] is. I know where to put my hands on her, and I shall have her before twelve o'clock." Then he left.

Grandma panicked. She went into action and contacted Old Betty. Betty responded by taking Harriet out of the closet forthwith and transporting her into the kitchen. She lifted up a wood plank in the kitchen floor, and Harriet crawled into the false space. The plank was lowered back in place. "Stay dar till I sees if dey know 'bout you," warned Old Betty. "Dey say dey vil put thar hans on you afore twelve o'clock. If dey *did* know whar you are, dey won't know *now*. Dey'll be disapinted dis time. Dat's all I got to say. If dey comes rummagin' 'mong *my* things, dey'll get one bressed sarssin from dis 'ere nigger."

As each intense hour passed, Harriet waited. She barely had enough space in front of her to place her hands over her eyes to keep the dust from falling in them as people walked through the kitchen. Old Betty cursed Dr. Norcom's name under her breath, knowing Harriet could hear her. It was her way to keep Harriet encouraged against her mortal enemy. Every now and then Betty would declare her confidence that Norcom would lose this battle.

With a chuckle, she would say, so Harriet could hear, "Dis nigger's too cute for 'em dis time" (*ILSG*, 132–33).

When Betty felt Harriet was in the clear, she secretly escorted her back into the more comfortable closet room. Betty concluded that Norcom's blustering was only a bluff to scare Molly. But a short time later, Harriet began intensely regretting Old Betty's conclusion, for suddenly she heard a familiar voice downstairs. It was a voice too dreadful, too terrifying, to be mistaken. Dr. James Norcom was in the house. Harriet knew it was over. The intelligence must have been real, the threat credible. She knew he had come to seize her at last.

Harriet braced herself against the wall of the closet as she heard footsteps walking up the stairs and into the bedroom. She knew it was Norcom and the constable. She felt faint as the key entered the keyhole. The door opened. She looked up.

"I thought you would hear your master's voice," she heard the calming tones of Martha Blount explain. Martha stood alone before Harriet at the closet door. "And knowing you would be terrified, I came to tell you there is nothing to fear."

Harriet just stood there, trying to catch her breath and reclaim her sanity.

Martha smiled. "You may even indulge in a laugh at the old gentleman's expense," she continued. "He is so sure you are in New York, that he came to borrow five hundred dollars to go in pursuit of you." Martha explained that her sister had made the loan to Norcom and that he was planning on leaving for the North that very night. "The doctor will merely lighten his pocket hunting after the bird he has left behind," Martha quipped.

The hidden laughs at Norcom's expense would only intensify when the depressed old malcontent returned from New York empty-handed, without a single lead to follow up on, and now in debt to Martha Blount's sister (*ILSG*, 134–35).

◆ ◆ ◆

One night, shortly after Norcom had returned from New York, something mysterious happened to Harriet while she was alone in her closet. A vision was laid out before her. She explained that, while everyone slept and the house was completely still, she lay there thinking about Joseph and Lulu. Right then she heard singing. It sounded to her like a "band of serenaders," and they were singing "Home Sweet Home." The singing sounded to her like the voices of children. She immediately sat up and got on her knees. "A streak of moonlight was on the floor before me," Harriet later wrote, "and in the midst of it appeared the forms of my two children. They vanished; but I had seen them distinctly. Some will call it a dream, others a vision. I know not how to account for it, but it made a strong impression on my mind, and I felt certain something had happened to my little ones."

Since many people lived in the Blount home, only Martha and Betty possessing knowledge of their secret guest, Harriet would have to wait until one of the two women came to her to confirm the vision. But they could only visit her when the house was clear of any potential informant who might ruin everything. So those closet visits were few and far between. The next morning Harriet received partial confirmation of the veracity of her vision, as she heard voices discussing some great news about Joseph and Lulu. But she could not ascertain the details. The anticipation was killing her. Harriet later remembered these tense moments, writing, "I bit my lips till blood came to keep from crying out." She asked herself in desperation: "Would Betty never come, and tell me the truth about it?"

Finally Betty came to the closet. At once, Harriet peppered her with questions and told her what she had gleaned from her hiding place.

"Lor, you foolish ting," Old Betty replied, "I'se gwine to tell you all 'bout it. De gals is eating thar breakfast, and missus tole me to let her tell you; but, poor creeter! t'aint right to keep you waitin,' and I'se gwine to tell you. Brudder, chillern, all is bought by de daddy!" (*ILSG*, 139).

This is what happened: When Norcom came home from New York empty-handed and in debt, someone was watching. It was the children's father, Samuel Sawyer, who had been waiting for this very opportunity. Sawyer knew from experience that Norcom would never sell him the children, so he secretly hired a slave trader to do his bidding. The slave trader was instructed to go to Norcom with a very generous offer for Joseph, Lulu, and John. Sawyer had given strict instructions to the trader to not reveal who the true buyer was. Dutifully, the trader made the offer to the depressed and indebted Norcom, telling Norcom he must have a bill of sale drawn up immediately because he had to get on his way. Norcom fell for it and took the deal.

After the deal was made, Norcom woke up to his true senses, remembered his love of revenge, and went back to the trader. He attempted to force an agreement with him that the children could not be sold anywhere in the state of North Carolina; he wanted to be sure Harriet would *never* see them again.

"You come too late," responded the trader. "Our bargain is closed." The trader then began rounding up his property, including the children and John, and loading them into his wagon. Norcom stood there powerless (*ILSG*, 136).

Molly's daughter Aunt Betty, who loved the children and had spent the first month in jail with them, came to the jail to say good-bye. Betty was the twin sister of Harriet's mother, and she had always tried her best to protect young Harriet from Norcom. The bond between Harriet and Betty was strong. But poor Betty would toil her entire life as a Norcom slave. Her only consolation was her husband, who was a seaman and a slave. He visited his Betty whenever his ship docked at Edenton. They had been together for twenty years and were truly in love. One day, for no apparent reason, Norcom came to Betty and forbade her from ever seeing her husband again. The couple obeyed and separated forever. With one command, Norcom had shattered her only light (*ILSG*, 272). From then on, Betty's sole remaining hope was to see Harriet free. "I shan't mind being a slave all my life," Aunt Betty once told Harriet, "if I can only see you and the children free" (*ILSG*, 165). And now, here Betty was at the jail, seeing that last dream die. Nobody had told her what was really happening.

Aunt Betty had to now fill the difficult role of substitute for Harriet. She had to be the children's mother in what looked to be the most difficult experience of their lives. When she got to the jail, she entered Joseph's cell. The six-year-old boy jumped into her lap and showed her how he had made marks in the cell wall, one for each day he had been locked up. Aunt Betty gazed upon the sixty marks in the wall.

Joseph broke the sad silence. He looked up at his aunt and declared, "The speculator is going to take me and [Lulu] away. He's a bad man. It's wrong for him to take grandmother's children. I want to go to my mother." Nobody had told the children what was really happening either. All Aunt Betty could do was hold the boy and love him as best she could for the last time.

As the children were being loaded up along with other purchased slaves, Grandma Molly showed up at the jail with a bundle of clothes for them. Grandma Molly had been told the truth about Sawyer's scheme, and she was asked to play along, which was why she brought the clothes. But as she said good-bye and watched the wagon pull out of town, the scene looked too real to her. She saw husbands and wives, children and parents, being torn apart forever in that moment. Family members in the wagon, and others in the street, fell down crying and moaning in despair. As she watched, she began to believe she had been deceived—that her babies were really being taken from her forever. She fainted in the street and was carried back home.

When she woke up in her home later that day, perhaps she thought she was seeing a vision. It was too good to be true! There before her, running with open arms, were her great-grandbabies Joseph and Lulu. Her grandson John was also there. They hugged. They kissed. They held each other tight (*ILSG*, 136–37). Sawyer had made good on his word. Even better, he had put the bill of sale in the name of Grandma Molly, which made her the legal guardian ("owner") of the children (*ILSG*, 222). Sawyer was also there at Molly's home, celebrating with his children. Though he never attached himself as a true father to his black babies, at least he had redeemed them from destruction. Per his instructions, the slave trader had carried the children and their uncle John just outside of town. There the trader released them. Another wagon was waiting to carry them directly back into town and into the bosom of Grandma Molly.

Harriet, of course, had missed all this, but she had been given a vision that very night that something grand had happened. Now she knew.

As Old Betty finished recounting the story to an over-whelmed, closet-bound Harriet, she concluded humorously: "I'se laugh more dan nuff, tinking 'bout ole massa [Norcom]. Lor, how he *vill* swar! He's got ketched dis time, any how; but I must be getting out o' dis, or dem gals vill come and ketch *me*." With that, Old Betty closed the closet door and went away laughing to herself.

Harriet was alone again. But she was now filled with a feeling she had not yet experienced. "Can it be true," she thought to herself, "that my children are free? I have not suffered for them in vain. Thank God!"

As expected, when Norcom found out he had been duped yet again, his anger and fury were beyond description. He began making threats against Harriet like never before—all his fiery verbal darts eventually getting back to the mother locked in the closet. Harriet had learned, for example, that Norcom had gone to Molly to renew his commitment to find and enslave Harriet forever, promising Molly that Harriet "shall be my slave as long as I live, and when I am dead she shall be the slave of my children." He also told Molly that if he ever saw John in the street and John "presum[ed] to look at me, I'll flog him within an inch of his life." Then, pointing to the children, he warned, "Keep those brats out of my sight!"

But his words had little effect on Harriet. "The darkest cloud that hung over my life had rolled away," she explained. "Whatever slavery might do to me, it could not shackle my children. If I fell a sacrifice, my little ones were saved." Norcom's threats, she said, "no longer had the same power to trouble me . . . it was the first time since my childhood that I had experienced any real happiness" (*ILSG*, 135–40).

◆　◆　◆

Norcom was at his wit's end. He could not find peace in Harriet's happiness. He doubled down. A rumor began that Harriet was hiding in Edenton. Many homes were searched, including the Blount home. Luckily, the searchers skipped the closet, but things were getting too hot. Harriet was rushed back into the kitchen and placed again under the plank. The stress, confinement, and dampness of the hard ground under the floor made her ill. She was taken intermittently back to the closet. At one point, while she was in the closet, someone was trying to get in. Several keys were tried, but fortunately none worked. As it turned out, the searcher was one of Martha's slaves, Jenny, who could not be trusted. She had likely heard movement in the closet, and—with the search for Harriet intensifying—thought she might be Norcom's hero.

It was clearly time for Harriet to leave. She needed a better hiding place. And the place chosen for her was Snaky Swamp.

Before Harriet left the house for the swamp, Old Betty brought her some sailor's clothes, in which she got dressed up. She was going undercover through the streets of Edenton. As she got ready, she tried to thank Old Betty for all she had done.

"I don't want no tanks, honey," she said. "I'se glad I could help you, and I hope de good Lord vill open de path for you. . . . Put your hands in your pockets, and walk rickety, like de sailors."

As Harriet entered the street below, she was met by a friend who had worked for her late father. His name was Peter, and Harriet knew he could be trusted. "Take good cheer," Peter told Harriet, "I've got a dagger, and no man shall take you from me, unless he passes over my dead body."

They made it safely to the water. Peter then rowed her deep into the swamp—at least three miles deep. After Harriet's earlier encounter with snakebite, she was naturally apprehensive. But she did not cower. Peter went with her and cut a path through the bamboo. He made a makeshift seat of bamboo and branches. Harriet took her position. She would spend two nights in the swamp. Her skin soon became swollen from mosquito bites, but the snakes were what terrified her the most. They were larger than normal snakes, and they attempted to crawl upon her all night, as she fought them back with a stick. "But even those large, venomous snakes," declared Harriet, "were less dreadful to my imagination than the white men in that community called civilized."

At the end of two nights, Peter came and began to row Harriet back to shore. He told her that a new hiding place had been prepared for her. Harriet could not imagine what or where this place would be. But she went forward with faith. As the boat landed back at Edenton, she got out, again dressed as a sailor. Her disguise was so good that, as she walked up the street, she accidentally came face to face with the father of her children. As she passed Sawyer, she brushed right up against his arm, and he didn't even flinch. He had no idea it was her. As Peter walked her the short distance up Broad Street, he told her, "You must make the most of this walk, for you may not have another very soon." They

Tim kayaking toward Snaky Swamp

turned left on King Street and approached Molly's home. Harriet entered and was immediately hoisted up through a freshly built trapdoor in the ceiling of the storage room. She would not come back out for almost seven years (*ILSG*, 141–45).

As Harriet crawled into her attic hiding place, she was instantly shocked at what she must endure now. Her new home under the slanted, shingled roof measured three feet high at its peak. She estimated it was no longer than nine feet, with a width of about seven feet. When she lay down and then rolled over, she would bump her head on the ceiling. With little air, and even less light, the place was hell on earth. And even though her life in slavery might not have seemed so bad to some, "Yet, I would have chosen [living in this attic]," she declared, "rather than my lot as a slave" (*ILSG*, 146–47).

If authorities were to find out that Grandma Molly was hiding Harriet, Grandma could, according to the law, be sentenced to death. With people coming to the house every day to purchase

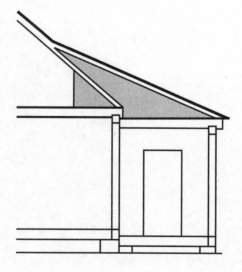

Grandma Molly's house, showing Harriet's hiding place (shaded area)

Grandma's baked goods, and with Norcom being so suspicious of Grandma and her house, it was imperative that Harriet never come out of her tiny space.

While in the crawl space, Harriet busied herself with reading the Bible and newspaper clippings her grandma snuck to her through the well-concealed trapdoor. The summers were very hot and the winters extremely cold. The extreme weather, and her inability to move her muscles, caused Harriet intense pain. Some days she would crawl around and around in her small space just to keep her blood flowing. Harriet also had to constantly fight off rats and small insects that bit her and made her skin burn. But she found some joy in watching her children.

Though she could not tell the children she was there (in case they accidentally revealed the secret to someone), she drilled a small hole in the wall, about one inch square, which allowed her to peer outside and watch them play in the street below. "Alone in my cell, where no eye but God's could see me," wrote Harriet,

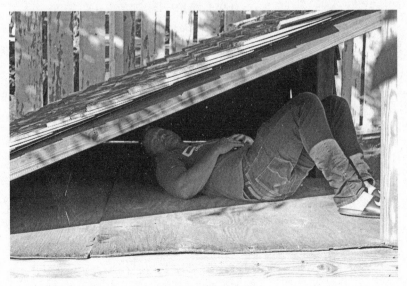

Tim lying in a replica, built to scale, of Harriet's secret attic space

"I wept bitter tears. How earnestly I prayed to him to restore me to my children" (*ILSG*, 170). But she refused to be helpless. Among other things, she managed to sew clothes and make toys for her children, especially for Christmas, which helped her feel connected to them while she waited for liberty (*ILSG*, 151).

"I suffered for air even more than for light," Harriet wrote. "It seemed horrible to sit or lie in a cramped position day after day, without one gleam of light. . . . But I was not comfortless. I heard the voices of my children" (*ILSG*, 147). "I tried to be thankful for my little cell, dismal as it was, and even to love it, as part of the price I had paid for the redemption of my children" (*ILSG*, 156).

SECRET SANTA

Little Joseph was in awe at the mysterious homemade toys and clothes made secretly by his mother, which would appear as gifts to him out of nowhere. One day Harriet overheard Joseph's friend tell him that Santa Claus isn't real and that Christmas gifts come from moms and dads. She smiled as she heard Joseph counter the claim, stating, "No, that can't be. For Santa Claus brought [Lulu] and me these new clothes, and my mother has been gone this long time" (*ILSG*, 151–52).

Aunt Betty would come to Harriet from time to time and give her news of Norcom's movements. On one occasion, Betty relayed to Harriet that Norcom, determined that Harriet was hiding in the North, was leaving once again for New York to hunt her down. He made the voyage and once again returned home empty-handed. Shortly after his return, Norcom was walking down King Street when he happened upon little Joseph standing at Molly's gate. Joseph had heard that Norcom had gone to New York to find his mother. "Dr. [Norcom]," he yelled out, "did you bring my mother home? I want to see her." Harriet was watching and listening from her hideaway. And yet she could do nothing when the old gentleman from Eden Street replied to the innocent inquiry by stamping his foot at the poor motherless child, exclaiming, "Get out of the way, you little damned rascal! If you don't, I'll cut off your head." The terrified boy ran into the house, yelling back, "You can't put me in jail again. I don't belong to you now" (*ILSG*, 149).

On other occasions, Norcom would try to appear kindly toward the children, hoping to trick them into revealing whatever they might know about their mother's whereabouts. Once, after trying to bribe them with toys, he asked what they knew. Lulu just hid herself from the monster. Brave little Joseph spoke up: "Dr. [Norcom]," he said, "I don't know where my mother is. I guess she's in New York; and when you go there again, I wish you'd ask her to come home, for I want to see her; but if you put her in jail, or tell her you'll cut her head off, I'll tell her to go right back" (*ILSG*, 149–50).

As the years went on, Norcom, ever desperate, began to make false claims that somehow the sale of Joseph and Lulu had been illegal, though he himself had taken the money for the children. He said the bill of sale was invalid because Harriet and her children actually belonged to his daughter, and only she could sell them. (Historical records proved him once again to be the consummate liar; he had made the estate of his daughter whole by purchasing two other slaves to replace the children he had sold.[14]) He was after Harriet's children. He wanted them enslaved.

In an attempt to thwart Norcom's efforts against her children, Harriet once again took a proactive position. Working through Molly and other friends, Harriet sent Lulu to New York with a family who agreed to take care of her there and send her to school. Sam Sawyer concurred with the decision and helped to facilitate the move, making arrangements for Lulu to move

MARY NORCOM STRIKES AGAIN

One day Harriet moved rapidly to her spyhole when she heard the terrified screams of little Joseph. He was being attacked by a fierce dog. Harriet saw her little boy covered in blood. Luckily, he escaped, and a doctor was called to clean and stitch him up. Harriet's heart ached as she heard her child cry and moan as he was being sewed up. She wished so badly that she could exit her attic and comfort her only son. But a smile soon found its place on Harriet's face when, a few moments later, Joseph stood and began threatening to avenge himself on the evil animal. The smile didn't last long, however, for a short time later, Dr. Norcom's wife, Mary, passed by the house. She saw that Joseph had been injured. Someone told her the cause. Mary then replied, "I'm glad of it. I wish I had killed him. It would be good news to send to his mother. Her day will come. The dogs will grab her yet." Harriet was forced to listen to these vile words as they passed through the mouth of the lady of Eden Street (*ILSG*, 157–58).

in with the family. Lulu was only about seven years old at this time, young for such a major transition. But, again, knowing the fate of little girls under the threat of slavery—especially Norcom slavery—Harriet would not risk her daughter's future happiness any further.

The night before Lulu left for New York, Harriet decided to reveal herself to her daughter. It would be the first time in many years that mother and daughter looked into each other's eyes. Late that night, Harriet slipped out of the crawl space and relocated to what had once upon a time been her bedroom. There she waited until she heard the little footsteps of Lulu, who had been

A MOTHER'S GOOD-BYE

"I took her in my arms and told her I was a slave, and that was the reason she must never say she had seen me. I exhorted her to be a good child, to try to please the people where she was going, and that God would raise her up friends. I told her to say her prayers, and remember always to pray for her poor mother, and that God would permit us to meet again. She wept, and I did not check her tears. Perhaps she would never again have a chance to pour her tears into a mother's bosom. All night she nestled in my arms, and I had no inclination to slumber. The moments were too precious to lose any of them. Once, when I thought she was asleep, I kissed her forehead softly, and she said, 'I am not asleep, dear mother.' Before dawn [Grandma Molly] came to take me back to my den. I drew aside the window curtain, to take a last look at my child. The moonlight shone on her face, and I bent over her. . . . I hugged her close to my throbbing heart; and tears, too sad for such young eyes to shed, flowed down upon her cheeks, and she gave her last kiss, and whispered in my ear, 'Mother, I will never tell.' And she never did" (*ILSG*, 178–80).

instructed to enter the room, not knowing why. Lulu opened the door and saw Harriet there.

"[Lulu], my dear child," Harriet spoke gently, "I am your mother." Lulu stepped back at first, trying to take in what she was experiencing. She then approached her mother and fell into her arms. Lulu raised her head and quietly asked, "You really are *my* mother?" Harriet reaffirmed who she was and then asked Lulu if she would like to stay with her all night before she left Edenton forever. Lulu was more than thrilled by the invitation (*ILSG*, 178–80).

Lulu was now safe. Somehow, some way, Harriet would figure out a way to get Joseph up to the North as well. And then, somehow, some way, she herself would escape and reunite with her little family somewhere in the free states.

CHAPTER 6

PORT-AU-PRINCE, HAITI, 2014

O.U.R. was now on the case to locate and liberate Gardy Mardy. We were headed for Haiti.

As the wheels of the plane carrying my team touched down at the Toussaint Louverture airport in Port-au-Prince, my thoughts turned back to a man named Levi Coffin. Levi Coffin was a white nineteenth-century businessman, Quaker, and abolitionist whose home in Newport, Indiana, served as one of the most successful Underground Railroad safe houses in America. Some even called his home, which was modified with a trapdoor and secret hiding spaces, the "Grand Central Station" of the Underground Railroad. It is believed that more than three thousand fugitive slaves passed through his care.

Levi was married to Catherine White, and together they raised six children. While Levi was busy running his businesses and engineering fugitive slave rescue missions, Catherine organized a sewing society to make clothing and prepare other necessary goods for fugitive slaves in need.[15]

Though his abolition career became renowned while he was living in the free Northern states, Levi Coffin cut his teeth in the dangerous practice of freeing slaves when he was growing up on his family's farm down in the Southern slave states. In fact, Levi was a contemporary of Harriet Jacobs and had grown up right in the heart of Harriet's state of North Carolina. It was there that

The Levi Coffin home

he encountered slavery for the first time. Levi was one of seven children, and the only boy, born to his Quaker parents—farmers who settled in New Garden, North Carolina. Young Levi would often tend to his hogs, who would run wild in the woods near his home. That was when he encountered runaway slaves, and his heart instantly went out to them. He approached them, listened to their stories, sympathized with them, and helped them. He would often stuff his bag with cornbread and bacon, then run it to the fugitives as they made their way north through the nearby woods. Word got around, and fugitive slaves began sneaking into Levi's room at night, pleading for help. He happily obliged.[16]

As Levi grew, he became more aggressive in his covert work. On one occasion, he learned of a North Carolina slave named Jack. Jack's master had died, and in his will he had set Jack free. But slaves like Jack understood that they lived under a broken judicial system and could not trust even the legal will and

Levi and Catherine Coffin

document of a dead white man. Believing his freedom may be only temporary, Jack acted quickly. He left his plantation and went to the Coffin farm to hide out.

Jack's premonition had been correct. The judge in his case, at the request of the dead master's relatives, voided the will and re-called Jack back into slavery. But the family did not know where he had fled to. They sent advertisements out offering reward money for Jack's capture. The Coffin family acted by sending Jack with Levi's uncle, Bethuel Coffin, to smuggle him into Indiana on his wagon.

During this same tense period, another slave, named Sam, had escaped his plantation and also made his way to the Coffin farm. The Coffin family learned that Sam's angry master had left his plantation in search of Sam. They also learned that the master had heard through the rumor mill that a man was en route on a wagon trail to the North with a runaway slave. The angry master mistakenly felt certain that the runaway on the wagon trail was his slave, Sam.

Levi, who cared about both Jack and Sam and desired freedom for them both, was very concerned. He knew the angry master would move north and find Jack. Levi feared that the master, after learning the slave was not Sam, would take Jack as a consolation prize and turn him in for the advertised reward. So Levi did what he needed to. First he hid Sam in an undisclosed location. Then he went undercover.

Posing as a bounty hunter specializing in runaway slaves (a common career for many a Southern adventurer), Levi caught up with the angry master. He befriended the master and offered him an abundance of liquor (which Levi did not consume himself), weakening the master's senses and making him feel kindly toward Levi. Levi promised to help him track Sam, who he agreed must be the slave on the wagon trail north. Within a couple of days, Levi and the master caught up to Jack and Uncle Bethuel. When the angry master learned the black man was not his Sam, he grew frustrated. But Levi—his new "friend"—was there to persuade him to leave Jack alone. After all, Levi had just received new intelligence on Sam. Excitedly distracted away from Bethuel and Jack, the master left with Levi in search of Sam. Of course, the "intelligence" was invented in the mind of Levi, who then took the master to an area of North Carolina in the exact opposite direction of where Sam was actually hiding out.

The plan was beautifully executed. Both Jack and Sam became free men. The master went home defeated. And Levi returned to his farm, a big smile on his face.[17]

People like Levi Coffin are one of the main reasons I named my foundation *Operation Underground Railroad* (O.U.R.), the operative word being *Underground.* I had learned over the course of many years that the only way to get slave children out of captivity was to go underground—to go undercover. We had to infiltrate the black markets of human trafficking in order to get the kids out. Now we were in Haiti for a reason, ready to employ our underground plan in order to rescue Gardy Mardy.

My team and I spent the next several weeks with the Haitian National Police, verifying several pieces of evidence that corroborated Guesno's suspicions that the orphanage he had identified was not actually an orphanage, but rather the home of a trafficking ring. This ring had managed to capture twenty-eight beautiful, innocent children, ages one to thirteen. Based on the evidence we had collected, one of these kids just *had* to be Gardy.

On the day of the operation, under the direction of the Haitian police, I was wired up with undercover audio and video devices. Our plan was to have me and another undercover operator pose as "buyers" in the trafficking market. We would simply knock at the door and talk our way in. If Gardy was there, we would identify him on our undercover cameras. If the traffickers offered to sell us children, we were instructed by the police to buy them in a sting operation. The police were grateful for our service, as they knew that our American faces would dupe the traffickers—for no American operator, to their knowledge, had ever gone undercover before working as an agent of the Haitian police. The traffickers would never see it coming.

The other reason our faces would be so convincing to the traffickers is the tragic fact that Americans represent a major portion of the demand for child sex slavery. In fact, the United States maintains one of the highest consumption rates of child pornography in the world.[18] Our faces worked simply (and sadly!) because traffickers were accustomed to serving Americans.

On the way to the orphanage, we dropped Guesno off at a

nearby hotel. His emotions were way too high for him to be at the target site. Our Quick Response Team (QRT)—made up of former Navy SEALs and other former U.S. Special Forces personnel, backed by Haitian authorities—waited in a van near the orphanage. Our communications were streaming live to the QRT. We had decided earlier on a distress code—a certain phrase that my partner or I could use to trigger the team to exit the van and breach the orphanage, violently if necessary.

My fellow operator and I were dropped off within walking distance of the target site. We approached the orphanage and identified its four large cement walls surrounding a courtyard and a few dingy outbuildings. I became sick to my stomach as I saw the words painted on the side of one of the walls certifying the place as a happy orphanage: an advertisement to the world, inviting innocent people to deliver innocent children there.

As we approached the gate, I took note of a few thuggish-looking individuals standing nearby. They eyed us with suspicion. Through the bars of the gate I saw a couple dozen children walking around glumly, dressed in raggedy clothing, some of them barefoot. Many of them had protruding tummies, and the whites of their eyes were noticeably cloudy and gray. We would later confirm they were all in the beginning stages of starvation. I also saw a man with a belt or small whip draped over his shoulder. I later learned that they called him "the teacher." He frowned at us as we peered through the gate.

This was it. Do or die. If they were selling kids, we just had to convince them that we were on their side, that we were in the market. *Their* market. On the other hand, if they found out who we really were, it could be the end of us quickly. This was our reality in that moment.

In the days and hours leading up to that moment, I had gone

through my preparation ritual for these types of undercover operations. I had been doing operations like this for many years now, and I had plenty of experiences to draw upon. And that's what I did. That was my preparation ritual. I would go over and over in my mind every operation I had conducted, reminding myself what I had learned. I would then apply these hard-earned lessons to what I imagined might go down as we entered these gates.

One lesson I had learned over the years was the importance of steeling my emotions against the sadness and tragedy connected to the children I was there to help. The child victims' horrifying stories were the kryptonite that might cause me to break down emotionally, fall out of character, and thus jeopardize the whole case.

The first time I recognized this was early in my career. I was investigating a case that required me to review hundreds of hours of child-rape videos. In an undercover capacity, I had been negotiating the transfer of the videos with one of the most prolific child pornographers I had ever seen, then or now. One of the videos from his collection depicted the severe abuse of three young children between five and seven years old—the same ages my children were at the time. But the real sucker punch was how similar the kids in the video looked to my own children—all three of them with blonde hair and blue eyes. I broke down at my desk in the evidence viewing station, fell to my knees, dry-heaved into the wastebasket, then picked myself up and ran out to the parking lot. I got into my car and sped over to the elementary school. I checked my kids out of school and took them home, where my wife was waiting for us. And then I just hugged them all until every tear in my body had left me.

Shortly after that case, I found myself in an even more emotionally damaging situation. One evening a windowless van was

attempting to make entry into the United States at the U.S.–
Mexico Port of Entry. The United States Customs and Border
Protection officer standing guard stopped the van and began interviewing the driver, a middle-aged white man. The officer also
identified a Mexican boy (we will call him Carlitos), no more
than five years old, in the van. Something was off. The officer
sent the van for secondary inspection.

Moments later my phone rang, just as I was sitting down
for dinner with my family. I was told to drop everything and
get down to the Port of Entry immediately. I left right away
and wouldn't return home for days. Turns out the man driving
the van was a pedophile and child pornographer. He had kidnapped Carlitos, who had been the subject of one of his child-
porn videos. The evidence we collected in the van led to multiple
warrants, including one for the Southern California home of the
predator, which was located several hours north of the border.
There we found his child-porn studio and identified close to a
dozen children whom he had taken and abused. Among the child
victims, we identified the thirteen-year-old sister of Carlitos.

After interviewing the sister, she asked me to visit her little
brother, who was residing in a government safe house near the
border where he was rescued. She wanted me to tell him she loved
him. I told her I would do it.

When I got to the safe house the next day, I approached the
boy, who was sitting in a small chair all alone. I pulled up a chair
equal in size to his, which was of course far too small for my adult
frame. I sat down awkwardly. We had spent hours together the
night he was rescued from the van, so we were already buddies,
and he was happy to see me again. There we were, sitting knee
to knee. I said nothing, just smiled. Then he jumped out of his
chair, ran over, and threw his arms around my head and hugged

me tight. He said in perfect, unaccented English, "I don't belong here." He then began to cry. I cried with him as the videos I had recently reviewed, which included depictions of this very boy, burned in my brain and broke my heart all over again.

He then pulled away, wiped the tears from his eyes, and pulled a little red Matchbox car out of his pocket and gave it to me. I didn't know why he had given me the gift, and though I tried to give it back, he insisted I take it. Before leaving, I told Carlitos I had seen his sister and that she told me to tell him how much she loved him. I also told him we were close to finding him a loving home, where he and his sister would be reunited. Within days, that had been done.

When I finally got home, I walked in the front door, saw my several kids running around as happy as can be, and I immediately broke down again, just like I had with the other case—and for the same reason. *My kids.* I instantly saw Carlitos's face in my kids' faces. *What if something so horrible were to happen to my kids? Why are they so lucky, while Carlitos and millions of others live in hell?* I couldn't shake the questions. I couldn't shake the fear. I couldn't shake the guilt, the grief, and the pain. My body literally couldn't bear it; my knees completely gave out, and I fell down. I sat crying like a baby on the living-room floor. My wife ran over and threw her arms around me. I hadn't slept in over forty-eight hours. I was exhausted physically and emotionally.

I knew in that moment that if I was going to move on in this work, I would have to steel my nerve. I couldn't let my emotional guard down ever again. Over the next months and years, I practiced. I trained my mind to prevent myself from ever associating the pain of child trafficking with my own children. It didn't resolve all the personal emotional problems inherent in this work, but at least I could continue in it effectively without going insane.

But as I stood before the Haitian orphanage gate that day, about to make undercover entry, I was having a change of heart about my emotional strategy regarding the kids in need of rescue. In fact, that change of heart had begun months earlier when I first met Guesno. The question he had asked me at the restaurant had never left me: "Could you get in bed and sleep at night, knowing that one of your children's beds was empty?" Guesno had unwittingly asked me to break the mental barrier I had spent years building. He had asked me to make it personal, and as a result I had quit my job to look for lost children!

I realized there was power in the question. Perhaps I had been wrong. Perhaps I should have found another way all those years ago to deal with my trauma. Perhaps I should have left my heart open to feel more, to let these kids into my heart more. Perhaps by so doing, I could have generated more passion, more power, and rescued more children.

As we began Operation Underground Railroad, and I studied more heroes from history, this new approach to the lost children—the "Guesno approach," as I call it—began making more and more sense. In fact, it appears as though these nineteenth-century heroes of light employed the same strategy.

Take Levi Coffin, for example. By his own account, the thing that had launched his abolitionist rescue mission was an event he had witnessed at age seven. He was near his family farm when he saw a group of slaves, shackled together in chains, being transported. He was astonished. He asked his father what he was looking at. His father explained slavery and told the boy that the men had to be shackled so they wouldn't run back to their families from whom they had been torn away. Levi's first reaction was the very reaction I had been running from for years: "How terribly we should feel," he recalled thinking, "if father were taken away from us."[19]

Harriet Jacobs had asked free people of the North—the very people she hoped would act on behalf of the oppressed and downtrodden—to consider that same question. She was tired of the brutal facts of slavery being hidden, downplayed, and averted. If free people couldn't be brave enough to face the darkness that attacked millions of innocent people around them (because it just hurt too much to know), then those poor, innocent victims would never have hope.

Harriet would see preachers and pastors from the North come to look at slavery in the South, but only the parts the slave owners wanted them to see. This is not unlike many of us who have heard of human trafficking today, those of us who glance at it but never really *see* it. Harriet asked these free people of her day the same question Guesno asks all of us in our day: "What [do they] know of the half-starved wretches toiling from dawn till dark on the plantations? of mothers shrieking for their children, torn from their arms by slave traders? of young girls dragged down into moral filth? of pools of blood around the whipping post?" (*ILSG*, 96).

I would try to change my perspective, and I asked my team to do the same. "These kids have nobody. They have no family," I told my team prior to the Gardy operation. "So we will be their family! We will make this personal." I also relayed to my team the advice Katherine had given me during the many years I had locked my heart, fearful of pain. "Whatever pain you feel," I told them, echoing my wife, "is nothing compared to what the kids feel." It helped me to remember that, and thinking of it helped me to engage dark things that were uncomfortable. Imagine if the whole world took these lessons to heart: how much suffering could be relieved?

With these thoughts, I opened the gate and walked into the orphanage. The man with the whip and a woman at his side— both with mean looks on their faces—approached us rapidly. We smiled broadly, which disarmed them. We explained to them that word on the street was that this was the place to get children.

The man and the woman looked at each other, then looked back at us. We continued to smile and act natural—like we did this all the time. They seemed to be buying it.

"Which kid do you want?" the woman asked.

Right then, I looked up and saw a very small child walk out of one of the dark outbuildings. He was wearing shoes about three sizes too big. He could hardly even walk in the shoes, but he seemed content to have them. He emanated a light I didn't fully understand, but I was instantly drawn to him. I allowed myself to open up emotionally, and my heart instantly melted for this boy. I channeled his light and my emotion and used them to empower me as an operator. I felt clearer and more mission-focused than ever before.

"I want that one," I said confidently, pointing to the small child. I walked over and knelt down next to the boy, who looked up at me curiously and apprehensively.

"What's your name?" I asked him.

He paused for a moment, unsure. Then, "Marky," he said shyly.

The man said nothing; he stayed back several feet from me at all times. The woman walked closer to me. She told me that she couldn't say anything else at this time, but that we should come back a different day to discuss details with their boss—the madam. She told us it was best to leave right away, that they did not want us there without the madam present. She gave us the phone number of the madam and told us to set up a meeting directly with her.

I quickly scanned the faces of the other kids, hoping my

undercover body camera would pick up Gardy somehow. I didn't believe I could identify him alone, and I quickly realized we would have to leave before we were able to see all the kids in this place, many of whom were walking around with their backs to us, while others were hiding inside the outbuildings. So as to not seem suspicious, we left as ordered. We would have to seek out Gardy another day. We told them we would call the madam and then return as soon as possible to negotiate the deal for Marky.

In short order, after having had several recorded phone calls with the madam, we made plans to return to the criminal orphanage in our same undercover capacity. After our briefing with the police, during which we reviewed the same protocols, procedures, and plans we had the first time we engaged the criminal network, we again dropped Guesno off at a nearby hotel and made our way to the target location.

As we approached the false orphanage, it was a very different scene. Instead of rags, the kids were all wearing school uniforms. It was clear the madam had these special clothes on reserve for when buyers visited her "products." Most traffickers call ahead, which was why our unscheduled visit had been so awkward the day before. The madam greeted us with a big smile. She too was wearing a similar uniform and, after shaking our hands, she began gathering the kids from around the yard. She lined them up in rows, shorter kids in the front, taller ones in back. She looked like a choir director organizing a performance. But the kids weren't about to sing. They were simply on display. It was an auction block.

I scanned the faces, looking for Gardy. I couldn't positively identify him.

The madam then escorted me over to the open door of one of the dark outbuildings. Looking into the outbuilding, she motioned with her hand, and Marky came running out.

"This is the one, right?"

I nodded.

I scooped Marky up in my arms, and he smiled at me.

My co-operator knew I needed to get into the outbuildings to search for Gardy and any other kids. So he called the madam over and began asking her questions. She was sufficiently distracted, and I made my way into the building. I was still holding Marky, trying to talk to him, pretending he was trying to show me something inside. In case someone was watching, this little ruse gave me some cover and made my entering the outbuilding less suspicious looking.

As I crossed the threshold, I was met by a stench that hit me like a brick wall. Urine. Feces. Rotting food. *How could children live in this?* I thought to myself. No amount of fake uniforms could cover the reality of what was going on here. As I entered deeper into the belly of the dark building, the sounds from outside—the adult voices talking, children whispering, cars on the street—faded to almost silence.

Only then could I hear what had always been there: the sound of small footsteps following me quietly, carefully.

I turned quickly, Marky still in my arms.

And there she was—a little girl. She looked to be maybe four or five years old. She was slightly larger than the boy in my arms. I immediately noted an open, infected, untreated wound over her right eye. I thought of the "teacher" and wondered if he had caused the laceration. She looked at me intensely. She was frightened.

I extended my hand to her, and she took it. Though I couldn't tell her the truth of what I was doing at the orphanage, I tried to let her see the pure intent in my eyes. She softened. I took a chocolate bar out of my bag and gave it to her, hoping it would calm her fears. She took it, without taking her eyes off of me or

Marky. She then did something I had never seen a child do before. Instead of taking the bar and running away, excited about
the priceless treasure she had lucked upon, she instead stood her
ground and broke the bar in half. It was almost like she did it out
of muscle memory. She then quickly handed half to Marky. This
was astonishing to me, as I knew that she, like the others, was on
the verge of starvation.

I put Marky down, and she immediately grabbed his hand
and held it tight.

"What is your name?" I asked.

"Mia," she said quietly but confidently, looking me square in
the eyes.

They were brother and sister. I knew it. I *felt* it.

Then it hit me. *Oh no!* I thought. *What have I done?* Of
course she was frightened. How many people had come to this
place, picking up a child in their arms like I was doing? How
many times? And how many of those children had then disappeared forever?

I knelt down on the dirty floor of this dark, creepy room and
took both their hands, the ones they weren't using to hold each
other. We formed a little circle. I looked Mia in the eyes and smiled.

"I'm your friend," I whispered to her.

She nodded. Somehow I could tell she believed me.

Having found nothing but shabby and broken beds, cribs,
and a few other pieces of old furniture in the dark building, I exited back into the yard, both children following behind me holding hands and eating their chocolate.

I consulted quietly with my operator, who confirmed that
the madam had made it clear—these kids were not up for adoption. They were for sale. She wanted fifteen thousand dollars for
Marky. She also wanted to consult with us on how we would be

extracting the child from the country; she wanted to school us on how we should evade authorities. He assured me that he had recorded the entire conversation for the police. I knew her days were numbered.

I then approached the madam. I asked her if the two children were brother and sister. First she denied it, evidently concerned that somehow this might affect the deal. When I pushed her on it, she finally admitted that they were, but that we could easily buy one without the other. They wouldn't care. There would be no problem.

Having just witnessed love between two children like I had rarely if ever seen before, I just looked at the woman. How could a human being get so cold, dark, and void of the ability to feel? All I knew for certain was that the only person in the world little Marky had was his sister, Mia, and all she had was him. I would not let them be separated. Ever. Not even for a short time. I promised myself this.

"Well, we need a boy and a girl, anyway," I said. "We will take them both."

As I said the words, I realized we didn't have enough cash on hand—but that wasn't going to stop me from keeping my promise to Mia and Marky. It was personal now. And I was happy it was.

We had agreed in the police briefing that if they were selling kids, we would do the transaction in one of the few luxury hotels in Port-au-Prince. The reason we gave the traffickers was that our cash was there; we also told them we wanted to exchange money in a very private place. The truth: wherever the money was exchanged would be the place of arrest, and the last thing we wanted to do was have a takedown scene at an orphanage, where scared kids might be caught in the crossfire.

We loaded up in a rented van, which was waiting outside the

gates of the orphanage. As we left, I scanned the large yard and compound one last time. I had not been able to look deeply into the faces of each child; I couldn't confirm that any of the kids was Gardy. But that didn't mean he wasn't there.

Now we had to focus on the operation at hand. Once we caught the madam and took down her operation, then we could dig deeper into the Gardy case, not to mention the cases of each and every one of the other kids. But first, we had to catch her red-handed. So we left the police to covertly stand watch at the orphanage while my operator, the madam, her assistant, the two kids, and I got into the van. The QRT would be tracking us in their own vehicles close behind. We headed for the hotel.

The madam put the kids side by side on the middle bench seat, while she and her assistant crawled into the back. My operator was toward the front of the van but sat looking backwards in order to keep his eye on all the occupants. I took the jump seat—a stand-alone seat that folded down near the sliding door.

Almost in the very minute that the van pulled away from the compound, Marky jumped up, a smile on his face, and hopped into my lap as if we were the best of friends or even family. He then immediately snuggled his little head into my chest and just relaxed. I wasn't expecting this show of affection. I was somewhat concerned that the madam would wonder why the "trafficker" sitting in front of her was cuddling the child and appeared to have a heart. But I figured she saw that Marky had initiated the connection, not me. Plus, she couldn't see my face. She couldn't see any proof that might betray my undercover persona. She couldn't see that I was starting to love this poor little boy.

We arrived at the hotel and moved the party to the presidential suite, which my team had rigged with multiple hidden audio and video devices hours earlier. We had ordered an abundance

Negotiating with the traffickers

of food, not so much for us or the traffickers, but for Marky and Mia. We knew they were perpetually hungry, and it was joyful for us to see them eat hamburgers and french fries until they were fully satisfied. It might have been the first time they had ever experienced such a thing as food satisfaction.

One of my operators escorted the children to the large, private balcony attached to the suite, where they happily played and ate more food. Then we got down to business with the traffickers. As we pulled out the cash requested for Marky—fifteen thousand U.S. dollars—we explained that we did not have enough with us at the moment to cover the cost of both children. We only had about twenty thousand dollars on hand. The madam agreed to let us pay her the remaining amount later. She explained the safest and most effective ways to smuggle the kids out of Haiti and evade police, sharing lessons she had learned from trafficking children out of the country successfully in the past. She also warned us that we could all go to jail if caught. I glanced up at the naturally placed audio speaker sitting on the bar. It was really a camera and recording device. I prayed it was picking up the madam's words, these final nails in her coffin.

Not once did she ask about our intentions toward the children. Obviously, there is no *good* reason to buy and smuggle children. No decent persons would smuggle children into their home, then raise them illegally, always wondering when they would be caught and investigated for kidnapping and harboring undocumented children. But for the madam, it was best she not know. So she completely avoided the subject.

Once the money exchanged hands, we quickly ended the meeting. We then escorted the traffickers out to the van, which was parked on the small, quiet street in front of the hotel. We told them that the van would be taking them home. But before we reached the van, three Haitian police vehicles rapidly pulled into place, trapping us from every side. We were all thrown to the ground (my operators and I were also "arrested" in order to preserve our cover), and the madam and her assistant were hauled off to jail in handcuffs. Mia and Marky remained (by design) on the private back balcony of the presidential suite during all this, completely oblivious to what was happening.

Once the criminals were out of the way, the police took our handcuffs off. It was now time to clean up the mess caused by the madam.

The Haitian police and child welfare workers were at the orphanage in short order. The "teacher" and other minions of the madam had somehow fled the place, never to be seen again. The police and welfare workers took the remaining twenty-six kids and prepared to transport them out to safe and secure aftercare homes. They worked to identify each and every one of the kids. Most of them, including Mia and Marky, were undocumented.

Without birth certificates, doctors literally had to guess their ages for the final report.

The police allowed one of my operators to accompany them to the orphanage and film the scene. The curtain was at last pulled back completely. It was worse than we thought. The conditions were unthinkable for these children. We saw babies in their cribs, wallowing in diapers that hadn't been changed in days. Feces and urine were spread across the place. The refrigerator was empty except for a bit of rotting food. There was really only flour and water in the kitchen, which made up the bulk of what these kids were being fed. (Months later, we learned that the doctors' age assessments for the children had likely been up to two or three years deficient. Once the kids starting eating properly for the first time, they began growing into their actual ages.) There was one room, and one room only, in the compound that was decent. That was the office and quarters of the madam, who also had a nice home of her own a few miles away.

As we drove in police cars from the hotel to the police station, Mia and Marky both on my lap, I was glued to my phone.

"Do they have Gardy? Have they found Gardy?"

That was the only question on my mind as I was getting updates from the police, accompanied by my operator, at the orphanage. They told me they would confirm the Gardy question as soon as possible. I still had no answer by the time we rolled into the police station.

Once at the police station, I took the kids into a private room that had been set up for us. We needed to be there in order to be fully debriefed as part of the prosecutorial procedure. Waiting for the kids in the room was more food, candy this time, and two teddy bears I had asked my team to provide for them. Mia and Marky were ecstatic. It was like Christmas for these kids. They grabbed their teddy bears and candy and jumped back on my lap. My heart was full.

The police live-streamed the interrogation of the madam into the room we sat waiting in. We listened on headphones. She tried to lie at first, then finally broke when confronted with the overwhelming audio and video evidence against her. When the police asked her about Gardy, she stiffened. She shut off and refused to say anything. There was nothing we could do; she wasn't going to budge on that one. She was in enough trouble as it was.

My phone rang. I answered immediately.

"I'm sorry, Tim," I heard the voice on the other end of the line say. My heart sank. That was all I needed to hear to know that Gardy was not there.

◆　◆　◆

I left the police station and went right to Guesno, who was still waiting in the lobby of a nearby hotel. He had spent the whole day praying, crying, and praying some more. For some reason, his cell phone hadn't been working all day, so we had not been able to get in touch with him at all. He still had no idea what had happened, no idea if we had recovered his son or not.

I walked into the hotel lobby all alone. There he was, sitting at a table. Our eyes met, and he knew instantly. Gardy wasn't at my side, holding my hand as I entered. That was the vision we had both played out in our minds hundreds of times in the weeks leading up to this point. And it hadn't happened. It wasn't going to happen. Guesno's shattered look was more than I could bear.

I sat down next to him. Neither of us could talk. He wept. I fought back tears.

"Tell me the truth, Tim," he said, breaking the silence. "They already sold him, didn't they?"

I wasn't brave enough to look him in the eyes. I just hunched over and stared at the ground—and nodded affirmatively.

About twenty seconds of complete silence ensued. Suddenly I was jolted up by the sound of Guesno slapping the table. I was shocked to see him grinning from ear to ear. That same mysterious light in his face emanated around his entire being, just as it had during our first meeting.

"But you rescued the twenty-eight kids, right?" he exclaimed, his eyes getting brighter.

"Yes, of course," I said, confused by his emotion.

"Tim, don't you see what happened? Those kids would never have been saved were it not for Gardy. If he had never been kidnapped, you and your team would never have come here. Those twenty-eight kids would still be slaves!"

I had never thought of it that way. I didn't know how to respond. I didn't know where Guesno was going with this. I just looked at him as he smiled and wiped tears from his cheeks. Then he said perhaps the most profound thing any human being has ever said to me:

"Tim, if I have to give up my son so that these twenty-eight kids can be set free, then that's a burden I'm willing to bear. I will make that sacrifice."

I was speechless. I wished I were half the man he was. I was humbled to be in the presence of such a great human being.

To prove he meant what he said to me, the next day Guesno marched down to the police station and volunteered to take any of those fatherless, motherless, abandoned children whom we had just liberated in his son's name. He went home that day with eight of them. He did this not knowing how he would pay for the enormous cost of raising eight additional kids. O.U.R. and other donors would eventually come to aid and support his selfless act of service for these children, but Guesno did not know that at the time. He just did what he knew he needed to do. Today, those kids all call him father, and they are all doing great.

After watching these events unfold, only then did I start to identify the magic that resides within Guesno Mardy. The lingering question I had had about this man, from the day I met him, at last was being answered. How does he keep the lights on—the smile, the spirit—while simultaneously living in the darkest hell any parent could imagine? The answer: he serves his fellow men. He serves, and the light can't help but follow.

◆ ◆ ◆

When I returned to the police station, I knew everyone would still be there. We had a lot of work yet to do. My entire team still needed to be debriefed. Mia and Marky needed to be interviewed. The evidence needed to be processed. I saw police officers busily working on all this as I walked down the hallway.

As I entered the room where I had left Mia and Marky, my heart sank. They weren't there.

"Where are they?" I asked one of my operators. "Are they still being interviewed?"

"No, they finished their interviews," my operator responded.

"Then where are they?" I asked, louder this time.

"The social workers took them to their new home."

"But I didn't even get to say good-bye," I shot back, as if my operator had somehow done something wrong.

I looked over to the corner of the room, and there sat the two teddy bears.

I sat down next to the teddy bears, exhausted, and put my hands over my eyes. I couldn't fight the emotion any longer. I was experiencing the burden and the blessing of opening my heart.

All that was before I knew how lost these two kids really were to me in that moment. It would be almost eight months of seeking, searching, fighting, praying, and scheming before I would find them and again look into their sweet little eyes.

OPERATION TRIPLE-TAKE

A Colombian child waits in a makeshift brothel,
minutes before being rescued from sex traffickers

On October 14, 2014, O.U.R., working together with Colombian and U.S. authorities, pulled off one of the largest single-day child trafficking rescue operations ever documented in history. By our simultaneously infiltrating multiple trafficking organizations in three Colombian cities, over 120 victims were rescued and more than a dozen traffickers and pedophiles were arrested, including at least one from the United States.

In the months following the operation, Colombian authorities and O.U.R. operators attempted to infiltrate other Colombian trafficking rings in the region, only to find that few if any were in operation. They had been deterred from continuing their illicit practices. Colombian authorities recognized that the deterrent power of Operation Triple-Take was having the desired result: in effect, children were being rescued who never knew, and would never have to know, that they needed rescuing, because their would-be abusers were now too scared to travel to them, and their would-be traffickers were now too scared to take and traffic them in the first place.

Due to the effective and highly coordinated effort of Operation Triple-Take, with agencies and aftercare partners spanning multiple countries and jurisdictions, this operation has become a principal case study in new legislation currently being considered in the U.S. Congress. The new bill—the proposed Hatch Anti-Trafficking Act—would formalize private-public partnerships in an effort to more effectively attack modern-day slavery.

CHAPTER 7

EDENTON TO NEW YORK, 1835–1852

I had a very painful sensation of coldness in my head," remembered Harriet, reflecting on her second winter in the crawl space, "even my face and tongue stiffened, and I lost power of speech." She fell into a state of unconsciousness, and her brother, John, and Grandma Molly believed she was near death. When finally she awoke, she was delirious—so much so that she could not control herself or her tongue. Molly and John feared she would betray her hiding place. So John, who had slaved away as Norcom's medical assistant and therefore had a knowledge of medicines, smuggled powerful drugs to Harriet to subdue her and keep her quiet. John also brought her herbs, roots, and ointments, which helped. He also managed to put some kindled coals into a small pan so that Harriet might feel something of heat. "Those few coals actually made me weep," Harriet remembered (ILSG, 156).

Such were the days and years of Harriet Jacobs during this difficult time in hiding. But she refused to just lie around. She was constantly working, scheming, plotting. In a daring act of psychological warfare, she wrote postdated letters to James Norcom and commissioned her confidant and seafaring friend Peter to take them to the Northern states (later, she even had a letter sent from Canada) and mail them back to Norcom's Edenton residence from there. She wanted Norcom to have further confirmation that

Harriet was indeed in the North. Peter, who had helped her hide in Snaky Swamp, was taking yet another significant risk for Harriet. "You may trust me," Peter told Harriet, upon receiving the request. "I don't forget that your father was my best friend, and I will be a friend to his children so long as God lets me live" (*ILSG*, 164).

The ruse worked. When Norcom got that first letter, he went to report it to Grandma Molly. He had forged a second letter to Molly, as if it had been written by Harriet. When Norcom came to the house to relay the forged message, Molly made sure he sat in a chair in a certain place where Harriet could hear the exchange. In the forged letter, Harriet had asked forgiveness of her grandmother for disgracing herself so badly in moving to the North and leaving her children behind. The letter also reported that Harriet was suffering greatly in the North and wanted to return to her old life. "It is very much as I expected it would be," declared Norcom after he finished reading and stood to leave. "You see the foolish girl has repented of her rashness, and wants to return." The lying and cunning man then asked Molly to help poor Harriet by sending a family member to the North in order to collect her and bring her home.

The old fool had become even more the fool (if that were possible). Harriet, hiding above him in the attic, forced herself to contain her laughter. "This was as good as a comedy to me," she later said.

Harriet had been victorious once again. The letters gave her the extra confidence she needed; she knew Norcom would not be looking for her in town anytime soon. In fact, the letters had largely shut him up, as he hardly even spoke of Harriet after that. This allowed Harriet to slip out of her hiding place more often so that she might exercise her body and limbs in the storage room

IRONY OF EDENTON

Edenton had been a prominent city during the American Revolution. Like Boston, Edenton had its own "Tea Party." Led by activist Penelope Barker in 1774, the prominent women of Edenton gathered and signed a petition to King George, stating their open rebellion and refusal to pay his taxes on tea and other items. It was one of the first organized political actions led and executed by women in the United States.

Penelope Barker's home stood a block away from where Harriet was holed up in Grandma Molly's home. Kitty-corner to Molly's home was a house once owned by Joseph Hewes, one of the signers of the Declaration of Independence. And the house directly adjacent to Molly's had once been the law office of James Iredell Jr., one-time governor of North Carolina and son of James Iredell Sr., who was appointed by George Washington to the post of Supreme Court Justice.[20] There sat Harriet among these symbols of liberty—while she had none. Though her country had betrayed her, she applied (most ironically) a famous revolutionary phrase to her own situation. She called it her motto. "Give me liberty," declared Harriet, "or give me death" (*ILSG*, 127).

Cannon from the American Revolution overlooking Edenton Bay, with Penelope Barker's home in background

below. She would need to restore her health as best she could if she was to successfully escape to the North (*ILSG*, 165–68, 181).

About this time, Harriet's brother, John, had traveled to the Northern states with Sam Sawyer, the lawyer who had purchased John out of Norcom slavery. And though Sam treated him kindly, and though John was grateful for the service rendered him, John still belonged to Sawyer and served him. One day, while in New York, Sawyer came to get John out of his hotel room so that they might return home to the South. But John was gone. He had left hours earlier. He simply stepped out onto the streets of New York and made himself free. "Some may try to make out of this a case of ingratitude;" John later wrote, "but I do not feel myself under the slightest obligation to any one who holds me against my will, though he starved himself to feast me.

. . . I have quite a friendly feeling for [Sawyer], and would be pleased to meet him as a countryman and a brother, but not as a master." Sawyer never even lifted a finger to try to get John back (*ILSG*, 277, 283–84).

Harriet was now encouraged more than ever to escape. Not only did she want to join her brother in the free states, but she still needed Joseph out of Edenton as well. John, now free, might

NOTE FROM JOHN TO SAM SAWYER

"Sir—I have left you, not to return; when I have got settled, I will give you further satisfaction. No longer yours, John S. Jacobs" (*ILSG*, 281)

be able to help with that. Strange things could still happen, as they often do in a slave society, which always tends to taint truth and justice. Grandma Molly could die. Sawyer could die. Norcom could sue for the boy. "It gave me a pang to look on my light-hearted boy. He believed himself free; and to have him brought under the yoke of slavery, would be more than I could bear. How

I longed to have him safely out of the reach of its power!" (*ILSG*, 182).

After almost seven years, at last an opportunity for escape presented itself. The bearer of the plan was none other than Harriet's loyal friend Peter. He came one night to the house. "Your day has come," he told her. As it turned out, Peter had made friends with a white sea captain. Though a Southerner, he despised the slave trade and was willing to help. He had a hidden cabin in his boat and offered to let Harriet hide inside as he delivered her to freedom. It was a small window of opportunity, as the captain would be leaving soon. "You have a fortnight to decide," Peter told her.

Harriet made preparations for the escape. Then, as is often the case when providential doors open, adversity attacked. The boat was delayed a few days, and precisely during those days, something terrifying happened. A fugitive slave known to Harriet and her family was captured and brutally murdered. Grandma Molly fell into a depression and saw it as a sign that Harriet would meet the same fate. Molly's sobs and groans of fear eventually caught hold of the otherwise brave heart of Harriet. Though it killed her to do it, Harriet ultimately abandoned her plan of escape.

Not wanting the opportunity to be lost, Harriet, the constant servant to the downtrodden, had an idea. There was a slave mother named Fanny who had found herself in a situation similar to Harriet's. Fanny had lost all her children at a slave auction, which drove her to run away. She had been hiding in the home of her mother ever since. The only reason Molly and Harriet knew of it was because little Joseph had seen her one day in her mother's home and had reported it to Molly. Harriet had Molly offer the opportunity to Fanny (*ILSG*, 191–93).

Fanny was shocked when she learned that Grandma Molly knew the secret, and she was anxious to take her chances on the vessel. Molly, of course, had said nothing of Harriet, who Fanny assumed had run to the North many years earlier. So Fanny was carried off by Peter and placed in the vessel. It appeared as though everything was going to work out for Fanny. But then a strong wind from the north hit Edenton Bay, making it impossible for the boat to move in the right direction. The next day was the same. Panic set in. With every day that went by, the chances increased that the boat would be searched. Fanny was at risk. Peter was at risk. And Molly was too. Molly feared that if Fanny were caught, she would be tortured and then confess all. Molly would be found out, and her house would be tossed and torn to pieces, exposing the even greater secret of who had been living in her attic for the past seven years.

As Fanny sat below deck inside the still-anchored boat, the pain caused by her fear must have been acute. She was relieved when she learned that the winds had finally shifted and the good captain had hoisted the sails. At last they were moving. But before they had made their way out of the bay, the captain looked over his shoulder to discover a boat being rowed rapidly toward him by two oarsmen. The boat carried a man whom the captain did not recognize. He was sure the jig was up—someone had snitched, the boat would now be boarded and searched, and Fanny would be discovered. It would be the ruin of all those who dared play such a dangerous game.

When the small boat at last caught up to the renegade vessel, a man sprang aboard. When the captain looked at him, he was as shocked as he was relieved. It was Peter.

"[There] is another woman I want to bring," Peter told the captain. "She is in great distress, too, and you shall be paid any thing within reason, if you'll stop and take her."

"What is her name?," asked the captain.

"Harriet," was Peter's reply.

What had happened?

As the boat sat anchored—Fanny hiding below deck and the captain waiting for a shift in the wind—the panic-stricken Molly had asked Harriet to slip out of the attic and console her face-to-face in the storage room below. Molly wrung her hands in distress as she predicted their ruin due to the delay in the boat's departure. She was so distressed, in fact, that she had forgotten to lock the door behind her. Suddenly she heard movement, and the door swung open. It was Jenny, the untrustworthy slave of Martha Blount, the one who had tried to get into Martha's closet room to discover Harriet some seven years earlier—one of the very few slaves in town who would betray her sister in a snap if given the opportunity.

Harriet ducked behind some barrels, but she was almost certain Jenny had laid her conniving eyes upon her. It was now only a matter of time before Norcom would know the secret.

Molly hurried Jenny out of the storeroom and into her bakery. As it turns out, Jenny had only come at the request of her mistress to purchase baked goods from Molly. Molly attended her, trying to act as natural as ever, after which Jenny left. Molly then returned to Harriet. "Poor child!" she exclaimed, "my carelessness has ruined you. The boat ain't gone yet. Get ready immediately, and go with Fanny. I ain't got another word to say against it now; for there's no telling what may happen this day."

At Peter's request, the captain had stopped the boat and waited for Harriet. Using the cover of darkness, Harriet would make her way to the wharf and out to the seabound vessel that very night.

But before she left, she had asked Molly to bring Joseph to see her. She had not held her child's hand, touched his sweet face, hugged him, kissed him, or even spoken to him since he was six years old. He was now twelve. Molly brought Joseph into the storeroom. Mother and son held each other and wept together. But Joseph was not so surprised by the revelation as Harriet would have expected. "I knew you was here," he told his mother, "and I have been *so* afraid they would come and catch you!"

Joseph explained that, years earlier, when Lulu was still there, he had heard a cough coming from the attic. Somehow he knew it was his mother's. He had also witnessed some things on the night Lulu left that made him believe she had met with their mother. He told his mother that whenever there were children playing on the side of the house where Harriet's crawl space was, he would coax them away and encourage them to play in a different area so that they might not hear the same cough he had heard. He also explained that whenever he saw Norcom chatting with policemen or patrols, he would hurry and report it to Grandma Molly. Astonishingly, he never told a soul—not Lulu, not Grandma— what he knew. He even proliferated and constantly gave credibility to the rumor that his mother was somewhere in the Northern states. He just quietly protected the secret and his mother. "I now recollected," Harriet later confessed, "that I had seen him manifest uneasiness, when people were on that side of the house, and I had at the time been puzzled to conjecture a motive for his actions."

Harriet knew she was pressed for time. She promised her boy that if he were good, honest, and loving to his dear grandmother, the Lord would open the way for him to one day come north to live with his mother and sister. Grandma eventually came in and took Harriet's hand. "Let us pray," she told her granddaughter. The three knelt down in the storeroom. Harriet put one arm around Joseph and pulled him in tight. With her other arm she embraced her grandma. "On no other occasion," Harriet later wrote, "has it ever been my lot to listen to so fervent a supplication for mercy and protection. It thrilled through my heart and inspired me with trust in God" (*ILSG*, 189–99).

As Harriet reached the wharf, about to step aboard the rowboat that was to take her to her escape vessel, she felt a gentle tug. She turned around, and there was Joseph. "I've been peeping into the doctor's window," he whispered, "and he's at home. Good by, mother. Don't cry; I'll come." Then he turned and ran back home (*ILSG*, 200).

Before long, Harriet was aboard the escape boat and embracing Fanny, who was beyond shocked to see Harriet step into her secret quarters below deck. "Harriet, can this be *you*," Fanny cried, "or is it your ghost?" The two friends sobbed so much over their reunion that the captain had to come and kindly remind them that they were both fugitives still in the South and that they needed to hush up.

As the boat made its way out of Edenton Bay and got far enough away from land, the captain gave the women permission to come on deck as much as they liked, so long as there were no other boats in sight. When they passed Snaky Swamp, the captain—no stranger to the Underground Railroad—pointed to it and said aloud, "There is a slave territory that defies all the laws." Harriet said nothing, but only thought of the terrifying nights she had spent there.

Ten days later they arrived in Philadelphia. Harriet was almost thirty years old, and she had at last made it to the free states! (*ILSG*, 201–3).

What a miracle the previous weeks had been! As it turned out, nothing ever came from old Jenny. She had most likely seen nothing in the storeroom that night after all—which, of course, only adds to the mysterious, miraculous chain of events that ended in this beautiful moment of arrival in Philadelphia. What if there had not been a weather delay once Fanny boarded the ship? What if Molly had not forgotten to lock the storeroom door? What if Jenny hadn't showed up unexpectedly? If any of those occurrences had not happened, then Harriet would still be locked up in an attic. Moreover, if the strange coincidences had not occurred that had led Harriet and Molly to suddenly abandon the opportunity for escape, then Fanny would have been left behind in dire need. And yet, all these things happened, and they combined to instead deliver two innocent daughters of God to the freedom they deserved.

IN HARRIET'S WORDS

"And how shall I describe my sensations when we were fairly sailing on Chesapeake Bay? O, the beautiful sunshine! The exhilarating breeze! and I could enjoy them without fear or restraint. I had never realized what grand things air and sunlight are till I had been deprived of them" (*ILSG*, 203).

Though they had arrived in Philadelphia at night, the captain advised them to stay on the boat and disembark in the morning, so as to not excite suspicion. Better to hide in plain sight. "Be it said to the honor of this captain," wrote Harriet, "Southerner as he was, that if Fanny and I had been white ladies, and our passage lawfully engaged, he could not have treated us more respectfully." Harriet remembered how the captain during their voyage had expressed embarrassment and shame toward his countrymen (to include his own brother, who was a slave trader) for participating in something as pitiful and degrading as the buying and selling of human beings. He would do what little acts he could to counter the evil (*ILSG*, 202–5).

The captain pointed Harriet and Fanny to elements of the Underground Railroad in Philadelphia. From there the women were cared for and set on their way. Harriet, at her request, was sent safely to New York City, where she went in search of her precious Lulu, whom she had not seen in two years. Only about seven when she had left her dear mother that sacred night in Molly's home, Lulu was now nine years old and somewhere in or near that great Northern city. Though Harriet had found immediate friends, she was saddened by the obvious racism and discrimination she also encountered in the North (*ILSG*, 209). She quickly realized that she had much work still to do to help change an unfair and crooked American system, even in the Northern states. She would fight until the end to do so. But for now, it was time to focus on finding her baby.

Once in the city, Harriet found a friend from her hometown who helped her track down the family with whom Lulu had been residing. Eventually they found what they believed was the right neighborhood. Shortly thereafter, they saw two young girls walking by them. Harriet immediately recognized the eldest of the two girls as the daughter of a woman who had been especially close to Grandma Molly many years earlier. Harriet was elated to see her and hugged her tightly.

"You take no notice of the other girl," Harriet's friend said to her. Harriet turned her head and looked into the younger girl's eyes. Her heart melted immediately. There before her stood Lulu. Harriet grabbed her and held her close. Lulu had grown and changed so much in two years. Though thrilled to see her daughter, Harriet was sad to see signs of neglect. The family had obviously been treating her more as a servant than a daughter, and they had failed to keep their promise to send her to school. Harriet would now make it all right. Once she got a job and saved up money, she would get Lulu out of her less-than-ideal situation. Harriet would work and fight to bring her family back together (*ILSG*, 210–14).

Harriet found a job in New York City as a nanny at the home of Nathaniel and Mary Willis. Harriet rapidly became a beloved employee of the family as she cared for their baby, Imogen. She was also able to keep an eye on Lulu, who lived not far away. Even though Lulu legally belonged to Molly, there was always the underlying fear that the corrupt legal system would reverse justice. What if the family that had Lulu decided to try to make a claim on her, even sell her? After all, they had not kept their promise to send her to school and were instead treating her as a housemaid. Harriet had seen stranger things happen. But perhaps more than Harriet watching Lulu, it was Lulu who needed to keep an eye on her mother—for she was an actual fugitive slave, with zero protection from the law, and Norcom was still out there.

Upon arriving in the North, Harriet also looked for her brother, John. She learned that he had gone to sea on a whaling expedition. She did not know if or when she would ever connect with him again. One day, while she sat looking out the window, she saw a black man walking down the street. He was wearing sailor clothing and analyzing every home on the street as he passed. Could it be? Harriet dashed out the door and jumped into the arms of her brother, who, after hearing Harriet might be in the North, had been tracking her down. They laughed and cried as they told each other of their respective adventures on their treks from slavery to freedom. They went to see Lulu and included her in the celebration. John stayed a week before heading back to his home base in Boston. "There are no bonds," wrote Harriet about the reunion, "so strong as those which are formed by suffering together" (*ILSG*, 217–18).

Unfortunately, Harriet's bursts of happiness seemed to be constantly countered by further challenges—and another challenge was on its way. It came in the form of a letter to Harriet from a friend in Edenton. Norcom was on his way to the North in yet another attempt at Harriet. The letter had been delayed, which meant Norcom could have already arrived. He could be very near indeed. Harriet had little time to pack her things and head further north to Boston in order to hide out. Luckily, she made it to Boston without incident.

Early one morning, while Harriet was hiding out in Boston, she heard a loud knock at her door. Someone was very anxious to get in. Had she been found out? The door swung open, and in ran the person who had been knocking so violently. Harriet approached the trespasser. When their eyes met, her heart instantly melted.

"O mother!" said her Joseph, completely out of breath, "here I am! I run all the way; and I come all alone. How d'you do?" Some friends from Edenton had sent the boy to New York; then, knowing where Harriet was hiding out, others helped to rush him up to Boston. "O reader," wrote Harriet of this surprise, "can you imagine my joy? No, you cannot, unless you have been a slave mother." Harriet joyed in her reunion and made every arrangement to integrate Joseph into Bostonian society.

Once she got word that Norcom had given up again and returned home, Harriet left Joseph in Boston in the care of her brother, John. She then went back to the Willis home in New York to resume her happy employment and to look after Lulu. The one drawback was her employers' request that she take the baby outside daily for walks and fresh air, especially during the summer months, when Southerners were more prone to travel. "Hot weather," declared Harriet, "brings out snakes and slaveholders, and I like one class of the venomous creatures as little as I do the other" (*ILSG*, 221–23).

Harriet was right to be concerned, especially when word got

to her that a man from Edenton, a Mr. Joseph Blount, had taken an extended stay at the home where Lulu lived. The family Lulu lived with naturally had ties back to Edenton, Sam Sawyer being the link that had introduced Lulu to them in the first place. And so, Mr. Blount's visit was not surprising. But it *was* dangerous, especially for Harriet. With Lulu in the house and Harriet nearby, it would be impossible to conceal Harriet's otherwise secret location.

Like Joseph, Lulu was bright, sensitive to danger, and fiercely protective of her mother. She sensed the darkness in Mr. Blount. She complained about his constant requests for her to go and purchase alcohol for him. When he got too drunk, he would ask Lulu to pour the liquor for him. But then it got worse, as he began spewing grotesque language into the small girl's innocent ears.

One day, while Lulu was outside sweeping, she saw Mr. Blount exit the house, tear up a letter, and litter the pieces onto the pavement. He then returned to the house. Lulu was suspicious. What letter had he written that was so controversial? Was it just a copy of an original he had already sent? Or was it a draft of a letter he was planning on finishing and sending later? Lulu quietly picked up the pieces and convinced children in the neighborhood (who could read better than she could) to help put the pieces together. The letter was written to Dr. Norcom, informing him of the location and address of Harriet Jacobs. The prize money was just too tempting for the immoral visitor from the South.

The first time Harriet had left quickly for Boston, she had made up a vague excuse for her good employer. This time she came clean. She told Mrs. Willis of her past: that she was a fugitive slave, and that she was in danger. Mrs. Willis was overcome with sympathy and called for her carriage. She immediately moved Harriet to the safety of a friend's house until Harriet's brother, John, could come and retrieve her. The family with whom Lulu lived understood why Harriet wanted Lulu to leave the city with her. They gave permission so long as Harriet agreed to return the girl in ten days. Harriet avoided making that promise. Instead, she would remove Lulu from New York with no intention of ever bringing her back.

Once in Boston, Harriet at last had her whole family together. It was a dream come true. "[It] was one of the happiest [days] of my life," wrote Harriet. "I felt as if I was beyond the reach of the bloodhounds; and, for the first time during many years, I had both my children together with me. They greatly enjoyed their reunion, and laughed and chatted merrily. I watched them with a swelling heart. Their every motion delighted me" (*ILSG,* 230–33).

As time went on, Harriet saved money in Boston and eventually sent Lulu to a boarding school for girls in upstate New York. As Joseph grew up, he desired to accompany his uncle John on a mining expedition to California. Poor Joseph had believed the Northern states would be free of prejudice. He was wrong. After Harriet placed him in a trade school, he was very well liked. On account of his mixed race, the other boys at first believed he was white. But when they learned he was black, they began to shun and persecute him. A pure soul like Joseph could not understand such ridiculous and wicked behavior—and so he was all too happy to take his chances in California (*ILSG,* 244).

Harriet, now alone in Boston, decided to return to New York, where she had more friends and opportunities. She stopped by the Willis home and visited the girl, Imogen, she had once cared for. Imogen had grown up, and it was a joy for Harriet to see her.

Sadly, Mrs. Willis had passed away years earlier, but Mr. Willis had since remarried a kind, aristocratic woman named Cornelia. Cornelia had recently given birth, and when Harriet was visiting the family, Cornelia asked if Harriet would like to return to the Willis home permanently as nanny to the infant. Harriet accepted.

During this otherwise happy time in Harriet's life, something horrific happened in the United States. Under Southern influence, the U.S. Congress passed one of the most wicked laws in its history: the Fugitive Slave Act (1850). In response to the Underground Railroad, which had helped thousands of slaves escape to the North, this law forced Northerners to assist in the capture of fugitive slaves, like Harriet, and force them back to their masters. The law also increased fines and promised jail time for those American Northerners who dared help, hide, or protect slaves from their masters. Government agents in the North assisted slave catchers from the South, and together they began rounding up fugitive slaves and sending them back to their nightmarish lives in chains.

Harriet wrote to a friend: "I closely observed the countenances of all I met. . . . I never [went] out in the day light. . . . There I sat, in that great city, guiltless of crime, yet not daring to worship God in any of the churches. I heard the bells ringing for afternoon service, and, with contemptuous sarcasm, I said, Will the preachers take for their text, 'Proclaim liberty to the captive, and the opening of the prison doors to them that are bound'? or will they preach from the text, 'Do unto others as ye would they should do unto you'?"[21]

Encouraged by the new law, Norcom doubled down. He started to hire private agents to hunt Harriet. She still feared for her children. Though Sawyer had purchased Joseph and Lulu

A WORD OF WARNING

CAUTION!!

COLORED PEOPLE
OF BOSTON, ONE & ALL,

You are hereby respectfully CAUTIONED and advised, to avoid conversing with the

Watchmen and Police Officers of Boston,

For since the recent ORDER OF THE MAYOR & ALDERMEN, they are empowered to act as

KIDNAPPERS
AND
Slave Catchers,

And they have already been actually employed in KIDNAPPING, CATCHING, AND KEEPING SLAVES. Therefore, if you value your LIBERTY, and the *Welfare of the Fugitives* among you, *Shun* them in every possible manner, as so many *HOUNDS* on the track of the most unfortunate of your race.

Keep a Sharp Look Out for KIDNAPPERS, and have TOP EYE open.

APRIL 24, 1851.

"It was the beginning of a reign of terror to the colored population. . . . Many families, who had lived in the city for twenty years, fled from it now. Many a poor washerwoman, who, by hard labor, had made herself a comfortable home, was obliged to sacrifice her furniture, bid a hurried farewell to friends, and seek her fortune among strangers in Canada. Many a wife discovered a secret she had never known before—that her husband was a fugitive, and must leave her to insure his own safety. Worse still, many a husband discovered that his wife had fled from slavery years ago, and as 'the child follows conditions of its mother,' the children of his love were liable to be seized and carried into slavery. Everywhere, in those humble homes, there was consternation and anguish. But what cared the legislators of the 'dominant race' for the blood they were crushing out of the trampled hearts?" (*ILSG*, 245).

and had given them to Molly, Harriet believed that if Norcom ever found them and kidnapped them back into the South, he could possibly get a Southern judge to nullify the purchase, especially since it was a black woman, Molly, who "owned" them. So when Harriet received a letter from the South informing her that Norcom had learned her address and even had descriptions of the Willis family members, her heart sank into her stomach.

Harriet turned to Cornelia Willis, hoping she might help. Cornelia didn't hesitate. In fact, she went above and beyond the call and helped Harriet prepare to move back to New England and hide out there. Then she proposed the unimaginable: She told Harriet to take her own infant with her to provide her extra protection. Harriet couldn't believe it, so she questioned Cornelia on the strategy. "It is better for you to have baby with you," Cornelia replied, "for if they get on your track, they will be obliged to bring the child to me; and then, if there is a possibility of saving you, you shall be saved." Harriet was dumbfounded. "But how few mothers would have consented to have one of their own babes become a fugitive," Harriet later explained, "for the sake of a poor, hunted nurse, on whom the legislators of the country had let loose the bloodhounds!"

One of Cornelia's family members, an aristocratic man of influence, told her she was crazy and that she was violating the laws of her country in helping to protect and hide a fugitive slave. He asked her if she did not understand the consequences of such

> ## A KIND ACT
>
> "Kind Mrs. [Willis] came to bid me goodbye, and when she saw that I had taken off my clothing for my child, the tears came to her eyes. She said, 'Wait for me, [Harriet],' and went out. She soon returned with a nice warm shawl and hood for [Lulu]. Truly, of such souls as hers are the kingdom of heaven" (*ILSG*, 232).

treason. "I am very well aware of it," Cornelia shot back. "It is imprisonment and one thousand dollars fine. Shame on my country that it *is* so! I am ready to incur the penalty. I will go to the state's prison, rather than have any poor victim torn from *my* house, to be carried back into slavery."

Harriet hid with the baby in the New England countryside for over a month. Finally, when Norcom's agents went away, Harriet came back home and resumed her work in the happy home. One day, she was watching as a boy in the employ of the Willis family was kindling a fire with old newspapers. Harriet realized that, being as busy as she was, she had forgotten to check the papers, which often published the names of out-of-town guests who had recently checked into hotels. Harriet stopped the boy just as he was about to send the paper into the fire. She took it and quickly began scanning the names. Two names immediately jumped out of the advertisement and sent fiery darts into her soul: Mary Matilda Norcom Messmore and her husband, Daniel Messmore. This was the Norcom daughter who technically owned Harriet. She was now married, and she and her husband had fallen upon hard times financially. They had come to New York to claim their prize and do that which James Norcom had failed to do—catch Harriet.

Harriet immediately informed Cornelia of the situation, and Cornelia sprang into action. Because Harriet had been delayed in reading the paper, nobody could be sure where the slave catchers were. They could be outside at that very moment. Cornelia called for her carriage and smuggled Harriet inside. They traversed the city, watching to see if they were being followed. When they knew they were in the clear, Cornelia dropped Harriet off at a safe house—a trusted friend's home.

Shortly thereafter, the lure began. People began showing up

at the Willis home, friendly looks on their faces, asking kindly for Harriet and Lulu. One person claimed to have a letter from Grandma Molly that he just *had* to deliver to Harriet in person. All it would have taken was a positive identification and the police could be called and, by law, would have to assist in the "legal" kidnapping. Thankfully, Harriet was not there. Cornelia instructed the household to respond to all inquiries the same way—*Harriet once lived here,* they told the visitors, *but no longer does, and nobody knows where she went.*

Harriet's friends gathered counterintelligence on the Messmore couple. They confirmed that the couple had every intention of grabbing Harriet's children. They were perpetuating the lie that Norcom's sale had been illegal because his daughter was the only lawful owner.

As things heated up, Cornelia worried and went to Harriet in her safe house. Cornelia pleaded with Harriet to move back to New England for a time. Harriet refused. She was tired. She was bitter. She was done. The only thing working on Harriet, however, was the fact that while Joseph was safe in California, Lulu happened to be on vacation from school and was with Harriet in the city. Cornelia sat patiently with Harriet, pleading with her and convincing her to endure this but a bit longer.

Harriet finally consented and agreed to climb into the carriage bound yet again for New England. Before she got in, Cornelia came to Harriet and again handed over her precious baby to protect the fugitive slave. Harriet, Lulu, and baby then set out for New England in a heavy snowstorm.

Cornelia would not stand for this injustice any longer. She rolled up her sleeves and went to work—she would end this misery once and for all. She hired a professional negotiator to approach the Messmores. Her agent convinced them that they could never catch such an elusive fox as Harriet. An offer was made. In return for Cornelia's payment of three hundred dollars, the Messmores agreed, bound by legal contract, to relinquish all claim upon Harriet and her children. The deal was done. Harriet, Joseph, and Lulu were at last out of harm's way.

When Harriet learned what Cornelia had done, an unimaginable load was lifted. Words could do her feelings no justice. *Free at last!* Harriet returned with the baby as soon as possible. "When I reached home," remembered Harriet, "the arms of my benefactress were thrown round me, and our tears mingled. As soon as she could speak, she said, 'O [Harriet], I'm so glad it's all over!'" Harriet could think of nothing but the many efforts of her family—her children's father, her Grandma Molly, her friends—to purchase her freedom. And for all their efforts, they could not. But now, how they all would be leaping for joy at this sight. (*ILSG,* 249–58).

◆　◆　◆

As happy and relieved as Harriet was in her newfound liberty, something still bothered her profoundly. "I am deeply grateful to the generous friend who procured [my freedom]," she wrote, "but I despise the miscreant who demanded payment for what never rightfully belonged to him or his. . . . The freedom I had before the money was paid was dearer to me," she continued, "God gave me *that* freedom; but man put God's image in the scales with the paltry sum of three hundred dollars" (*ILSG,* 250–57).[22]

Harriet recalled a man who congratulated her one day on her freedom, declaring proudly, "I have seen the bill of sale!" Harriet had plenty to say about this thought, innocent as it might have been out of the mouth of the gentleman. She declared:

"'The bill of sale!' Those words struck me like a blow. So

HARRIET'S THOUGHTS ON CORNELIA WILLIS

"The noble heart! The brave heart! The tears are in my eyes while I write of her. May the God of the helpless reward her for her sympathy with my persecuted people. . . . God had raised me up a friend among strangers, who had bestowed on me the precious, long-desired boon. Friend! It is a common word, often lightly used. Like other good and beautiful things, it may be tarnished by careless handling; but when I speak of Mrs. Willis as my friend, the word is sacred." (*ILSG*, 250, 258)

I was *sold* at last! A human being *sold* in the free city of New York. The bill of sale is on record, and future generations will learn from it that women were articles of traffic in New York, late in the nineteenth century of the Christian religion. It may hereafter prove a useful document to antiquaries, who are seeking to measure the progress of civilization in the United States" (*ILSG*, 257).

CHAPTER 8

DARING ESCAPES VIA
THE UNDERGROUND RAILROAD

Harriet Jacobs finally found her way to freedom after years of trying, and her story inspires our efforts today to end the evil of slavery. But hers was not the only escape or the only inspiration for Operation Underground Railroad. The stories that follow, representative of many others, illustrate principles of planning carefully, of working together, of thinking creatively, and of acting with courage—all ideas that inform our work.

We begin with one of the most amazing slave escapes in American history. The year was 1862, and the country was in its second year of the Civil War. Twenty-three-year-old slave Robert Smalls, who had been forced in his youth to work as a seaman, had been tapped to serve as pilot and aide aboard an armed Confederate military transport, the *CSS Planter*. After weeks of scheming and plotting, Smalls and his little band of fellow slaves pulled off the unthinkable. At about 3:00 a.m. on May 13, while the white officers slept onshore, the black rebels seized the *CSS Planter*, which was docked in Charleston Harbor.

With its massive guns on board, and with Smalls donning a captain's hat and jacket, he steered the steamer due north through Confederate-controlled waters. En route, he stopped off at a pre-planned point, where he picked up his wife and two young children. Passing a gauntlet of heavily armed Confederate forts (all of which were duped by Smalls's disguise), he brought the boat

Robert Smalls

CSS Planter

safely through the Union blockade without incident, where he turned the *Planter* and its massive arsenal over to Union troops. He and his family were free at last.

Robert Smalls was lauded as a hero and given an award by the U.S. government. He was also given a commission as boat pilot under the Union command, where he served through the rest of the war. He was eventually made the first black captain of a U.S. Army ship. That ship was the refurbished steamer formerly known as the *CSS Planter*. After the war, he moved back to his home state of South Carolina, where he was elected to the House of Representatives. He also purchased the large home where he and his mother had once toiled away in slavery.[23]

Another story of ingenuity and courage is that of Henry Brown, who was born into Southern slavery in 1816. As a young man he was sent by his master to labor in Richmond, Virginia. He was married to a slave girl named Nancy. Henry worked on the side in order to pay Nancy's master to not sell her and their three small children.

One morning, Henry woke up in his small home like he did

every day, kissed his wife and kids good-bye, and headed to work. Unbeknownst to him or his family, Nancy's master had betrayed them all. He had sold Nancy and the kids. With Henry out of the house, the patrols came in and took away his family. By the time Henry got word, all he could do was show up on the street and witness his pregnant wife and three babies tied up in wagons with more than 300 other recently sold slaves, all being carted away to unknown locations to toil under new masters.

"Father! Father!" he heard one of his children calling to him from a wagon full of children who had already all been separated from their parents. All Henry could do was watch and cry, knowing he would never see that child again in mortality. Another wagon followed close behind. There he saw his Nancy. He ran to her and grasped her hand. "I went with her for about four miles hand in hand," Henry later wrote, "but both our hearts were so overpowered with feeling that we could say nothing, and when at last we were obliged to part, the look of mutual love which we exchanged was all the token which we could give each other that we should yet meet in heaven."

After his great loss, Henry decided he would escape slavery once and for all. As he toiled one day, he prayed that God would show him his escape route. Suddenly an idea flashed in his mind. Working with elements of the Underground Railroad, Henry would hide himself inside a box and have a friend mail it to abolitionists in Philadelphia. After purchasing a wooden crate (three feet wide and two and a half feet high), he acquired sulfuric acid and dumped it on his hand until it burned a hole down to his bone. This got him out of work for a time so he could work on his escape. He bored small holes in the box, then jumped inside, taking with him some water and biscuits. On March 29, 1849, the box was sent in the mail.

The box was carried by wagon, railroad, and steamer as it made its way north. At one point, while the box awaited a ferry, a postal worker left the box upside down. For over an hour, Henry was stuck head down. Just when he felt overwhelming pressure in his head, his eyes ready to burst from their sockets, he felt a cold, unnatural sweat cover his head. He took that as a sign of his imminent death. He then prayed one last silent prayer to God for deliverance. Right then, a man, complaining that he had nowhere to sit, turned the box right side up, which afforded him and another man more room. Henry was at last relieved of the indescribable pressure. The men rested on the outside of the box and chatted while Henry slowly recovered inside the box in total silence.

Eventually the box made it to the Philadelphia destination, where abolitionists were secretly awaiting it. "The joy of the friends [waiting in Philadelphia] was very great;" wrote Henry, "when they heard that I was alive they soon managed to break

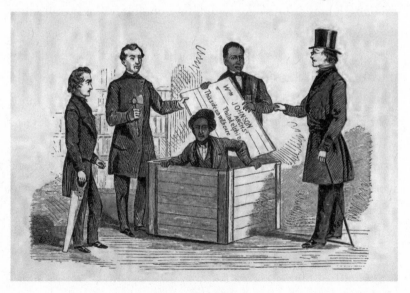

Henry "Box" Brown

open the box, and then came my resurrection from the grave of slavery. I rose a freeman, but I was too weak, by reason of long confinement in that box, to be able to stand. . . . But as the kindness of Almighty God had been so conspicuously shown in my deliverance, I burst forth into . . . [a] hymn of thanksgiving."[24] From then on, he was known as Henry "Box" Brown.

Note the elements at work in Henry's escape: his own courage, the help of friends to send and receive the box, and the apparent intervention of divine providence to get the box turned right side up. The careful planning of this operation led to his reward of being free.

Similar planning was evident in the story of Ellen and William Craft. In 1820, Ellen was born a slave in Georgia. She was the daughter of a slave mother and her mother's white master. Ellen was thus born with light skin, something she would eventually take advantage of to secure her liberty. She was also a house slave, which allowed her access to information about the area in which she lived. This was another point she would take advantage of.

When Ellen was twenty years old, she married a slave named William Craft. William had lost both parents and his fourteen-year-old sister after their master had separated each of them and sold them away. William and Ellen decided they would never raise a family under such conditions. So they patiently schemed and plotted against the demon slavery.

They decided to have William save up money to buy high-end men's clothing, including a top hat, cravat, jacket, tartan, and tassel. But the clothes were not for him. He gave them to his wife, Ellen. With her naturally light skin, her fancy new men's clothes, and her short hair (which she cut off as part of the ruse), she would attempt to pass as a white slaveholder. William would act in the role of her slave. They would travel to the North under these pretenses. Because the couple was illiterate, Ellen would put her arm in a sling, so that she had an excuse for why she could not write. She would also feign an illness to avoid having to speak. In December 1848, they began their daring trek.

The plan worked! Traveling by train and boat, their undercover tools and tactics allowed them to avoid detection. They arrived in Philadelphia on Christmas morning. News of their creative escape spread, and their masters learned what had happened and where they were. They sent agents to the North to recapture them. William and Ellen were forced to flee to the safety of England. There, five children were born to them. Their dream of raising a family in freedom had been realized.[25]

One final story holds special interest because it parallels perhaps more closely the situation with modern-day slavery. It involves a young man who was not a slave to begin with, but who found himself trapped in the web of evildoers, similar to thousands of people who are kidnapped and trafficked in our day.

In the early nineteenth century, Solomon Northup, a freeborn black man was thriving in New York State. He owned a farm and was a professional violinist. He was married to the love of his life, a free black woman named Anne Hampton, and they had three beautiful children.

One day in 1841, when Solomon was thirty-two years old, he was approached by two white men who wanted to hire him as musical talent in their production and take him on the road. Solomon jumped at the opportunity. Since some of the venues were scheduled to be in the South, Solomon was careful to secure the proper documentation proving he was a free man. He then willingly went with the men.

But Solomon was betrayed in the worst of ways. Once the men had Solomon in the South, they drugged him until he passed out. Then they took his papers, called him a fugitive, and sold him into slavery. There he toiled away on several plantations, where he was beaten and abused for more than a decade. Whenever he tried to explain the truth of what had happened to him, or whenever he claimed to be a free man, the abuse tended to get even worse. His wife and children were left without a clue as to where he had gone.

During his twelfth year in slavery, Solomon had a chance encounter with a white, Canadian contractor on the plantation. The Canadian man was Samuel Bass. Solomon had overheard Bass express his abolitionist views and decided to confide in him. Solomon quietly told Bass about his real identity and provided him contact information for his friends in the North. Bass acted on it. Solomon's friends couldn't believe it. They informed Northern officials, and an investigation was opened. Government officials verified the story, tracked down Solomon, and extracted him from slavery. At last, he was returned to his wife and children in the North.

Though his kidnappers were eventually hunted down and arrested, in the end the unjust "justice" system acquitted them of any wrongdoing.[26]

Today, tens of thousands of children, freeborn children, are taken and forced into slavery under false pretenses and loopholes in laws and customs. Such is the current fate of Gardy Mardy. Such was almost the fate of Mia and Marky and their twenty-six companions. And so it goes in the rest of the world. These patterns are repeated on every continent and in every country.

I suppose it's true what they say, *the more things change the more they stay the same.* I suppose we can, very unfortunately, repeat Harriet's words: all this evidence before us regarding modern-day slavery will "prove a useful document to antiquaries, who are seeking to measure the progress of civilization in the United States" and the rest of the world.

So what do we do? What *can* we do? We exercise all our ingenuity, creativity, and courage, as demonstrated in the stories above. We learn from the brave men and women who assisted slaves to escape through the Underground Railroad in the nineteenth century. We follow the examples of Mariana, Guesno, and the thousands of other freedom fighters in our day—the modern-day abolitionists, the modern-day slave stealers. We take what we learn and we fight back. We take what liberty we have been granted—whether through our own fight or through the fights others took on for us and before us—and we stand up for those in need.

Nobody did this better than Harriet Jacobs. Enduring to the end didn't mean just freeing herself. Rather, to her, it meant freeing all the others as well. This broader rescue mission would require joining hands with other abolitionists and taking on an American political system that had only preserved and protected slavery. And I'm not just talking about the obviously upside-down politics in the South. Northern states, along with the government of the United States, were complicit in this evil as well. Indeed, the U.S. government had made its position clear to Harriet and her colleagues by, for example, passing and enforcing the Fugitive Slave Act in 1850. Then, in 1857, the Supreme Court further protected slavery in the Dred Scott ruling, which barred any constitutional protections to people of color.

This is what Harriet and her colleagues were up against. But they would fight anyway. They would fight tooth and nail until justice was served and the wicked system was defeated.

CHAPTER 9

PORT-AU-PRINCE, HAITI, 2014–PRESENT

I was the only one still awake in the run-down hotel room in Port-au-Prince. My operators, exhausted after the long day of taking down the criminal organization that had sold us Mia and Marky, were out cold. Some were on the hard floor with blankets, others were sharing the two beds that sat side by side against one of the walls. I looked at my phone. It was 1:30 a.m. I kept hearing a rat dart across the room, jumping in and out of holes that lined the walls. One of our SEALs had tried to catch and kill the rodent earlier in the evening, but to no avail. We were all too tired to hunt the thing, which was why it was so frustrating that I could not sleep. I knew I was exhausted. I became irritated at the rat and blamed it for the fact that I was still up.

But it wasn't the rat.

It was the kids. All of them. It was the twenty-eight we had rescued. It was the one we had not. It was Guesno and his incomprehensible sacrifice. It was the words he had told me in the hotel just hours earlier, "If I have to give up my son so that these twenty-eight kids can be set free, then that's a burden I'm willing to bear." The bittersweet thoughts of all of this filled me, blessed me, haunted me.

But of all the thoughts keeping me up, the most prominent ones were those of Mia and Marky. I had allowed myself to love them. I replayed in my mind every scene with them. I saw Marky

147

pop out from inside the dark outbuilding, that moment I first saw him and felt something. I saw Mia breaking the candy bar in half and placing it into the little hand of her brother. I saw Marky in my lap, cuddled up to me, looking out the window, mesmerized by his first car ride. His ride to freedom.

But something else had happened on that ride. It was the most powerful memory of the day, and the one that kept me awake that night more than any other. As Marky had sat in my lap during the van ride, he had turned his head and looked into my eyes. He then reached up toward my neck and pulled a dogtag necklace off over my head. I was surprised he had even seen it, as it was hanging inside my shirt, leaving just a small part of the chain exposed. But he did see it, and he took it and placed it over his own small head. Being way too big, the necklace immediately fell over his shoulders. The very natural, casual way in which Marky had transferred the necklace (as if it had always been his, and I had just been borrowing it) made me smile. His act complete, Marky then turned his attention back to the window, cuddled back up into my chest, and continued watching the rapidly passing scenes of the downtown Port-au-Prince landscape.

That dogtag necklace wasn't just any necklace. It was a replica I had made of a nickel-and-dime store, plastic necklace, worthless in terms of monetary value, and yet it meant the world to me. Remember the story I told earlier about little Carlitos, the five-year-old boy whom we had helped liberate from the American trafficker and child pornographer on the U.S.–Mexico border? Well, the toy Matchbox car wasn't the only gift I walked out with in the wake of that investigation.

During the course of that event, I learned that Carlitos and his thirteen-year-old sister, also being victimized, had a prayer. They prayed they would be rescued from the evil that was attempting to conquer them, forcing them into one of the worst forms of slavery the world had ever known. This cheap, plastic necklace had represented that prayer. It was like some sort of rosary for them, and Carlitos had given it to me. Though I tried to give the necklace and the toy car back before we parted, Carlitos refused. I even tried giving the tokens back to the caregiver at the safe house. She said they were mine.

I put the necklace in my office, where it sat for many years. When the idea of Operation Underground Railroad began entering my mind, as I strove to put off the risky proposition, something providential happened. My ten-year-old son happened upon the necklace and brought it to me. He asked about it, and I told him what I could, what I thought was appropriate for a kid his age to know about the case.

"It's pretty cool that the little boy put your name on the necklace," my son said.

"What are you talking about?" I responded. "My name is not on the necklace."

My son handed it to me and pointed out the fine print at the bottom of the plastic trinket. My son was right, kind of—printed there on the necklace was a biblical reference: 1 Timothy 6:11. I had never noticed it before. But it made sense. This was the children's prayer. Now it became *mine.* Call it luck, fate, God, angels—whatever it was, it meant something to me, and it gave me power to make the difficult decision to leave my stable job in the government and start my foundation. I vowed to wear the necklace on every O.U.R. mission from that day forward. I eventually had replicas made of the necklace so my team members and I would always have one available to wear (and so I would not lose the precious original on an operation).

And so, when Marky pulled the necklace off my neck and

placed it around his little body, I became emotional. After years of successfully carrying out various roles as an undercover operator, in this instance, I almost broke character.

But the tears I had fought back on the van ride earlier that day had eventually, finally found their way out. They now flowed down my face and onto my pillow as I lay there in the middle of the night in a rat-infested Port-au-Prince hotel room, thinking about those two beautiful children.

Though I knew I had made this decision before the operation—I had agreed to open my heart—in my late-night moment of weakness now, I regretted it. I didn't want the pain. I didn't want to worry about the plight of Mia and Marky. I had to convince myself that all would be well and they would somehow find a loving home through Haiti's legitimate orphanage system. But I couldn't. So long as I saw their little faces in my mind's eye, I simply couldn't.

I rolled over and got on my knees. I would pray and plead with God to help me detach. I couldn't reasonably be expected to form these kinds of bonds with every child we helped. That would be hundreds, even thousands of kids. God had helped me with this before. I hoped He would do it again.

But He didn't. In fact, He made it worse. The more I prayed, the more I saw the kids. The more I felt. The more it hurt.

I jumped off my knees and ended the prayer immediately. The anxiety was building.

An irrational thought (no doubt brought on by my anxiety) entered my mind: *Since I'm not getting the answer I want through prayer, maybe my wife will have a better answer.*

I called her and woke her up. "I'm having an anxiety attack," I told her. I had her attention.

"The two kids I told you about. I can't stop thinking about

them. I can't stand the thought of one of our kids being stuck in a Haitian orphanage."

Confused, Katherine interrupted, "Wait, what do you mean by 'one of our kids'?"

I didn't know what to say.

"Do you feel these kids are part of our family?" she asked.

"I guess so," I replied. We both thought silently about a brief and vague conversation we had had earlier about the chances of us ever adopting—formally or informally—children we would rescue.

"Then go find them," Katherine said. "Let's *be* their family."

Katherine always has a way to simplify things that seem really complex to my sometimes confused mind. Though I didn't know exactly what she meant, I knew what I needed to do. The next day I went down to the police station and asked them to take me to Mia and Marky. I was shocked at their immediate response. After assuring me the kids were in a fine and secure place, they told me their laws prohibited anyone outside the system from knowing where they were.

"But I'm the one who rescued them!" I declared to anyone who would listen. It didn't matter. The law was the law, and I respected them for adhering to it. The police did, however, tell me that there was one person, appointed by the president, who could make an exception to the law. She was the director of the child welfare system for all of Haiti. I needed to make an appointment with her to plead my case.

And I tried. I tried again and again. Emails. Phone calls. No response. I showed up repeatedly at the child welfare headquarters. The director was never there when I was. Weeks passed, then months, and I couldn't find my kids.

After eight months had gone by, the stress became unbearable. My six children back home were aware of the situation and were also becoming frustrated. Having heard me tell at least part of the story, they were touched, and they now considered Mia and Marky their sister and brother.

"If you are an expert at finding kids, Dad," they would tell me regularly, "why can't you find Mia and Marky?" *Ouch!*

By this point I had become desperate. I was searching for something, anything, to help me. I thought of the people of light I had tried to emulate: Guesno Mardy. Harriet Jacobs. The original Underground Railroad. All of them gained light through prayer. They asked God. They hoped for the miracle. It was time to follow suit.

I was heading back to Haiti on a separate operation, but I was determined not to come home without having located Mia and Marky. With the powerful imagery running through my head of Harriet Jacobs kneeling in the cemetery, or falling to her knees after jumping out of the Norcom window, I felt compelled to ask my wife and children to do the same. I told them I would be going back to the child welfare offices the next day (which was a Monday) at 10 a.m. Port-au-Prince time. That would be 8 a.m. for Katherine and the kids. At that precise hour, even as I walked through the gates and into the welfare offices, I had to know they were all on their knees praying for Mia and Marky. I had to have that imagery in my head, knowing it was real. This time, something was going to happen. Something *had* to happen.

I approached the gate of the child welfare offices at 9:56 a.m. I stopped at the gate and took a deep breath.

The welfare office stands in the middle of a busy commercial zone of Port-au-Prince. Apparently, it had been a fashionable Caribbean-style, multilevel mansion in Haiti's heyday, back when tourists had visited the island in droves, before severe corruption had bred severe poverty, which had then bred severe slavery. Today the mansion is surrounded by walls and a metal gate guarded by government officers. Beyond the gate are a courtyard and a small parking lot, which lead to the offices themselves. I had been to this place many times before, asking, pleading, even begging to get a meeting with the director. But I had always failed.

"Tim, what are you doing? Let's go in," one of my operators said to me a bit impatiently. He couldn't understand why I was still standing outside the gate.

I looked at my watch. It was 9:58.

"I'll go in at 10 a.m.," I told him. My tone was serious enough that he didn't question me further. I didn't feel it was appropriate to share my reasons, to tell him or anyone else about how my wife and children, a couple of thousand miles away, were two minutes from dropping to their knees. It felt too sacred to me at the moment to mention. So I just stood there in silence. I wouldn't move until I knew they had.

At 10 a.m. I opened the metal gate. As I pushed on it, I felt someone behind the gate pulling. Perhaps one of the guards had heard us outside and decided to facilitate the opening so as to confront us immediately and proactively, to ask us who we were and what we wanted. But the face that appeared as I looked through the opening gate was clearly not a guard. Rather, it was an elderly, gray-haired woman, a Haitian woman whom I had never seen before. I had no idea who she was, and she didn't know me. She was holding a few folders in her hand and was exiting the premises.

I'm not sure what came over me next. I was so amped up for this moment—so sure something was bound, even destined, to happen at 10 a.m.—that I lost some of my composure. Without thinking, I grabbed the woman's arm (more forcefully than I should have) and exclaimed loudly in English, "Who are you?"

Few people in Haiti speak English. The fact that I would blurt out a question in English to this innocent, unassuming stranger, I can only explain by my full confidence that a miracle was about to happen, and when it did I wasn't going to miss it.

The woman naturally pulled away from me. She stepped back, then looked me sternly, bravely in the eyes, and responded, "Well, who are you?" *She speaks English,* I thought to my myself. *What are the chances?* And, of course, her question was more than reasonable, especially considering my inappropriate approach.

"I'm sorry if I startled you," I said.

Her eyes softened a bit.

"I'm looking for my kids," I said. "My two kids." She raised an eyebrow, confused.

I stammered: "Well, they aren't really my kids. They are Haitian children. But I want them to be part of my family, and I can't find them anywhere." I couldn't believe how stupid and mysterious, and maybe even a bit suspicious, I must have sounded to her.

But instead of balking, her eyes softened further. She spoke: "What are their names?"

Doubt set in for a moment. *How could she know?* I thought. *There are more than 30,000 orphans in the country, and only one person authorized to talk about them. And this woman is not that person.* I looked down at the ground and closed my eyes for a second, just enough time to kill the doubt with the simple yet powerful image of Katherine kneeling in prayer with our children.

"Mia and Marky," I responded. "At least, that's what they called themselves."

I hadn't even finished the sentence before I saw her eyes grow wide as they filled with tears. She instantly threw her hands in the air and began shouting and singing, "Praise Jesus! Praise Jesus!"

I stood there shocked, confused. She went on praising the Lord for a while. The awkwardness of the moment was drowned out only by my intense curiosity. Her spontaneous song of praise was beautiful, and I fully agreed with the sentiment, but I really, *really* needed her to expound.

"I know where your kids are!" she said finally as she lowered her hands.

I held my breath. Everything around me seemed to freeze in time.

"You are the one who rescued them!" she said, pointing at me, tears still flowing freely down her cheeks.

I was speechless. I could only nod in the affirmative.

"Twenty-eight children!" she exclaimed.

"Yes," I whispered, still stunned.

"Outside the Petionville hotel!" she said, her voice getting louder with each new refrain.

"Yes!" I said, this time in a full voice.

I now knew that she knew. Words can't describe the warm comfort that filled my soul.

"You know!" I said, as I took her hand in mine.

"Yes!" she said, still ecstatic. "And guess what?"

I opened my eyes wide and leaned in, as if to say *What? What?* She seemed to like the anticipation she created for me.

"I don't even work here!" she said, as she laughed out loud.

"But, how . . ." I didn't even know how to formulate my question.

She laughed and laughed, her joy adding to my own.

"Let me explain," she said, sensing my profound confusion. "When those children were rescued eight months ago, they were brought right here. They were divided into three groups, each group to be taken to a different orphanage. My orphanage just happened to be one of them. I was here. I saw Mia and Marky. I know which orphanage they were sent to. It's my friend's place."

I was out of breath—and again, I was speechless. I let go of her hand and placed both my hands over my face and rubbed my eyes as I tried to process all this.

"You see," she continued, "I just happened to be here this morning picking up some paperwork. I'm not here often." She got closer to me and took my hand. She got serious. "Do you realize," she asked softly, "if you had come through this gate even three seconds before or after you did, we would have missed each other? Three seconds and I would have been lost to you in the busy street outside. Lost forever."

I gained enough composure to finally put a coherent sentence together in response. "Well, do you realize," I said, my voice cracking and tears now forming in my own eyes, "that in the very moment I was walking through this gate, my wife and my children were on their knees, praying for this very miracle?"

"Ahhh," she said. "Yes, a miracle it is!"

She took her phone out of her purse and called her friend to explain what had just happened. She then hung up and told me to return the next day to this very place, to this very gate. My children would be here.

I returned to the sacred gate the next day at the appointed time. When I stepped in, Mia and Marky were standing in the courtyard. They looked so healthy. It seemed as though they had aged by at least two years. It's amazing what something as simple as food can do for a child.

At that moment, I felt so grateful that in this case, our strike on the false orphanage had had a preventive effect. Although these children had certainly been neglected and mistreated, they had not yet been subjected to the horrors that would have followed once they had been sold. As "goods" on the auction block, they were kept relatively unspoiled to make them more marketable. Because we got to them before traffickers did, we were able to spare every one of those precious twenty-eight children, including Mia and Marky, from a much worse fate.

Mia looked up at me. Our eyes connected. Instantly, she smiled and ran toward me. She threw her hands in the air.

"Papa Blanc! Papa Blanc!" she exclaimed as she jumped into my arms. (*Papa Blanc* means "White Daddy." I later called Katherine and jokingly told her that our new little kids may not be too politically correct.) Marky followed close behind and also jumped into my arms.

We sat down and talked about everything they wanted to talk about. Mia did most of the talking. She asked me all the questions she hadn't had a chance to ask before. "Tell me about your family"; "Tell me about your kids"; "What's America like?"

I pulled out my family Christmas card from the previous holiday season. Mia took it out of my hand before I could even explain what it was. With both kids on my knees, I pointed to each of my children in the photo and told them their names. As I said their names, Mia repeated the strange sounds until she could pronounce the names in English. She repeated back to me each of the names in question format (James? Sam? Delsy?) until I confirmed that she had it right. She quickly had each of my six children's names memorized. When I got to Katherine, Mia didn't say her name. She just caressed the depiction of her face and smiled. Marky watched the whole scene with interest, but he said very little.

When it was time to go, I promised them I would come to visit soon. Mia asked to keep the photograph. I told her it was hers forever.

The director of their orphanage then took their hands and began to exit the gate. I stood back and tearfully watched them leave, these poor children who scarcely knew what a loving family was. They had no memory of their late family. They didn't know what it was like to sit on a mother's lap and be sung to, read to, cuddled, snuggled, and just loved unconditionally.

Suddenly, Mia stopped, broke her grip with her caretaker, and came running back to me. She whipped the photo out and pointed to Katherine. With her finger squarely on Katherine's face, she looked into my eyes. There was inspiration and pure light in those beautiful brown eyes that I would come to comprehend perfectly in the coming months and years as I really got to know this special little girl.

"Mama Blanc," Mia said softly, her finger still on Katherine's face.

She was not asking a question.

PART 2
THEY CALL US
TO ACTION

CHAPTER 10

HARRIET TUBMAN—THE "CONDUCTOR"

After a decade and a half of running point on undercover operations, my team has slowly been convincing me that it's time for a change. My wife agrees. Fearful that my face has possibly become recognizable to too many criminal organizations (notwithstanding the superb makeovers our volunteer Hollywood makeup artist can apply to my face), I find myself today in a much more executive role. This affords me greater opportunity to speak to the public about modern-day slavery. It has allowed me to ponder over the subject and meet amazing people who help me comprehend better the problems and solutions connected to this societal plague.

One evening I was doing just that. I was speaking to a large group of influential and philanthropic-minded people about the problem. I had been invited to a beautiful home to give my presentation. Halfway through, the front door opened and a man walked in. I had been giving my presentation in a room adjacent to the home entryway, which gave me a direct view to the front door and the man who had just walked through it. My eyes immediately met those of the latecomer, and I was instantly taken aback. Perhaps a little starstruck. It was Burgess Owens, former starting safety for the world champion Oakland Raiders. I instinctively looked at his hand and identified the big, shiny Super Bowl ring on his finger.

Nobody had told me Burgess would be coming, nor did I even know he was living in or visiting the vicinity. I had never met him before and had no idea how or why he might have heard of me. It was a complete shock, further fueled by the fact that I had recently seen him on a major national news show where he appeared as a commentator. As he found an empty seat toward the back of the room, he smiled and nodded at me.

At the end of the presentation I made a beeline for him. I had to know what had brought him there this night.

"Tim!" he said, before I could get a word out. "Thank you so much for what you do! When I heard you were in town, I traveled quite a ways to see you. I've been following your activities for a while."

Confused and curious, I shook his hand and said very little. I was all ears.

"There is a story I have to tell you," he said as he gave me his card. "But it's too extensive to explain here."

He glanced around the busy room, where people were chatting loudly and munching on the refreshments provided as part of the event that night. His eyes told me that the story he had to share was important, perhaps even personal—and this was *not* the setting.

"Call me, and let's get together soon," he said.

I emailed him the next day, and he immediately followed up by sending me several historical documents telling the story of a man—his great-great-grandfather Silas Burgess. I learned that Silas Burgess was born in 1848 in Africa. He was only a child when he and his mother were kidnapped and forced into the belly of a slave ship bound for America. They were then sold to a South Carolinian planter with the last name of Burgess. Master Burgess was ruthless and beat and raped Silas's mother. When Silas was only eight years old, his mother was so tortured she could not go on. She ran away and was never heard of again.

"Grandpa Burgess was only a boy when he decided to follow his mother's example and flee to freedom," Burgess told me a few days later while sitting in my office. He wanted to tell me in person the rest of the story about his great-great-grandpa.

"But how could a mere boy make such an escape?" he asked. The answer was the Underground Railroad.

Burgess went on to explain how Silas took the lesser-known "underground" route that went into Texas and Mexico. He told me of how the boy had to be rescued several times from drowning in swamps as the group made their way through the Deep South and into freedom. Silas, who had only known white people to be brutal and horrifying, was now seeing something different: working hand in hand with the black operators along the secret route were white people and people of other nationalities and ethnicities. German-Americans were helping him. Mexicans were helping him. They risked life and limb to serve this fugitive slave boy born in Africa. The child was astonished. And the experience would shape the rest of his life.

"And this brings me to why I traveled the distance to meet you the other night," Burgess said. "I want to say thank you! Thank you for resurrecting the memory of the Underground Railroad. There is power for good in that name and memory. That power for good has traveled for generations and landed on me. It has touched my heart and it has touched my soul."

He went on to explain that Silas Burgess was so deeply affected by what he had seen along the Underground Railroad that he decided to do something about it. If people of different colors and varying religious beliefs could reach beyond societal pressures and prejudices and put service to others above all else, then so could he. After marrying and establishing himself as a free man and successful entrepreneur in Texas, Silas dedicated his life to serving others. He and his wife had eighteen children, and they founded one of the first churches in their community, which they named "Zion Hill." Zion Hill doubled as a grade school for children. The Burgess family had created a vehicle whereby they and the community at large might serve God's children in various ways.

Burgess then pointed out that for generations thereafter his family has followed that pattern of service to others. His own father would earn a PhD in Agricultural Science, then move for a time to Africa, when Burgess was a boy of only five, to help modernize food-growing systems there.

"It was a long and complex cycle beginning with Silas from Africa to America, then to my father who took us from America back to Africa again," Burgess said with a smile. "But it's a legacy of sacrifice and service that our family has benefitted from. And the legacy was largely born of the Underground Railroad!" (I would later learn how real this legacy was to Burgess Owens. After his NFL career, he and his wife raised their six children and dedicated their lives to serving others in various capacities. For example, today Burgess serves as a chapter president of One Heart Project, a nonprofit mentoring service for at-risk youth.)

Without skipping a beat, and without moving his head, Burgess pointed his finger back behind him directly to a portrait that hangs prominently on my office wall. He hadn't mentioned the portrait when he had come into my office an hour earlier, nor did I see him looking at it, but clearly he had made note.

"Look at her watching us," he said, still pointing behind his head at the portrait but looking at me square in the eyes. "My hero Harriet Tubman!" He continued, "The thing about that woman—she kept going back. Again and again. Back into the South. Back into danger. If she could just rescue one more, she would go back again. Why? Why did she do it? Nobody knew she was doing it. Few even knew who she was at the time. She had no motive but love. And look how much good came of it! This is the power of service!"

"I couldn't agree more," I responded to Burgess. "She is my hero too! Which is why her likeness hangs on my wall where I can see it every day." I went on to explain how Tubman and the Underground Railroad gave us so much of what we needed to launch our current rescue mission.

As Burgess stood to leave my office, he looked over at the portrait one last time. "She is our light in the darkness," he said, "and we need that light now more than ever. It's the magic of service."

After Burgess left, I sat back down at my desk, alone in my office, looking at the portrait of Tubman. I thought of what Burgess had just taught me about the true legacy of the Underground Railroad. I turned my head to see a large poster hanging on my wall, a gift from an anti-trafficking organization that had been following and helping to promote the relationship between O.U.R. and the Pittsburgh Steelers. It was a collage of photos depicting Coach Mike Tomlin and members of his team along with a photo from an O.U.R. rescue operation. Every member of the Steelers team had autographed the poster, which had the words *Slave Stealers* printed across it. As recounted in his foreword to this book, Mike had introduced me to these same lessons that Burgess had just delivered. How interesting (and really cool!) that these messages were largely pointed out to me by two men who were both Super Bowl champions. But way more interesting and

LETTER FROM FREDERICK DOUGLASS TO HARRIET TUBMAN

In 1868, Harriet Tubman had asked Frederick Douglass for an endorsement related to a book about to be published about her and the Underground Railroad. This was Douglass's response:

"Dear Harriet: I am glad to know that the story of your eventful life has been written by a kind lady, and that the same is soon to be published. You ask for what you do not need when you call upon me for a word of commendation. I need such words from you far more than you can need them from me, especially where your superior labors and devotion to the cause of the lately enslaved

of our land are known as I know them. The difference between us is very marked. Most that I have done and suffered in the service of our cause has been in public, and
I have received much encouragement at every step of the
way. You, on the other hand, have labored in a private way.
I have wrought in the day—you in the night. I have had the
applause of the crowd and the satisfaction that comes
of being approved by the multitude, while the most that
you have done has been witnessed by a few trembling,
scarred, and foot-sore bondmen and women, whom you
have led out of the house of bondage, and whose heart-
felt, 'God bless you,' has been your only reward. The midnight sky and the silent stars have been the witnesses of
your devotion to freedom and of your heroism. Excepting
John Brown—of sacred memory—I know of no one who
has willingly encountered more perils and hardships to
serve our enslaved people than you have. Much that you
have done would seem improbable to those who do not
know you as I know you. It is to me a great pleasure and
a great privilege to bear testimony for your character and
your works, and to say to those to whom you may come,
that I regard you in every way truthful and trustworthy.

> "Your friend,
> "Frederick Douglass"[27]

cool than that was the joint message they bore. *Service* turns the lights on in the darkness! It's the great healing ointment.

Suddenly, everything made sense. I continued to look around at all the art and photos that surrounded me in my office. It was the same message everywhere I looked. These things inspired me, but until now, I didn't fully realize why. I walked over to a picture of Mia and Marky. *They are the light in the darkness,* I thought. I walked over to another picture hanging on my wall of me and Guesno Mardy—*he is the light in the darkness!* I continued to scan the room. I saw several photos of Abraham Lincoln. *The light.* I saw Harriet Jacobs. *The light!*

Each of these great teachers of service had unique insights and special experiences that helped me to do my job—insights and experiences that could help our country heal. I felt so grateful to them all. As I stood there acknowledging each teacher's contributions, I followed my train of thought past all of them back to its conductor, Harriet Tubman. Although she had not had an Underground Railroad to conduct for more than 150 years, her memory and lessons continue to conduct us today toward liberty, harmony, and healing. I silently thanked her at the foot of her portrait that day for her example and leadership. I then turned toward the next stop in the train of leaders around my office and embarked on a journey to learn what each of them had to teach me. My first stop was Abraham Lincoln.

CHAPTER 11

ABRAHAM LINCOLN

Abraham Lincoln was born on February 12, 1809 (four years before Harriet Jacobs was born). He was born in a log cabin to a poor farmer and his wife. When Lincoln was nine, his beloved mother died. Not many years later, his sister, perhaps his best friend in the world, also died. Someone ran to tell Abe what had happened. A neighbor described what followed: "I'll never forget the scene. He sat down in the door of the smoke house and buried his face in his hands. The tears slowly trickled from between his bony fingers and his gaunt frame shook with sobs."[28] Lincoln's childhood sadness did not end there.

Lincoln felt it was his calling to learn to read and to study. But his father Tom did not like it, as it interfered with his farm work. He was cruel to Abraham and beat him.[29] Perhaps these early experiences taught Abe to be compassionate to those who suffered. He felt deeply for others who experienced misfortune. Even suffering animals gained his sympathy. He would stop other kids who abused animals for fun. He once told his stepsister that "an ant's life was to it, as sweet as ours [is] to us."[30]

As a young man, Lincoln got a job that required him to visit the South. He found himself walking the streets of New Orleans, where he came upon a slave market. He saw men and women chained up. He saw a young black girl being sold. He watched as slave owners walked up to her and poked her, prodded her, pinched her, and grabbed her mouth to look at the health of her teeth. They treated her like an animal they were considering buying, forcing her to trot up and down the street to test her strength and endurance. Lincoln was stunned. He turned to the young friends who were traveling with him and declared, "By God, boys, let's get away from this. If ever I get the chance to hit that thing, I'll hit it hard."[31]

How was it that Lincoln managed to get his chance to "hit" slavery? More important, when his chance finally came, what convinced him to act on it?

Lincoln would be given his chance to hit slavery by the dedicated abolitionists of his time, including Harriet Jacobs. Even before Cornelia Willis had arranged for her freedom, Harriet was already doing what she could to fight back against the parts of the American system that preserved and protected slavery. In 1849, after seeing Lulu off to boarding school, she moved to Rochester, New York, in order to help manage the Anti-Slavery Office and Reading Room—a place where people could go to learn the truth about slavery. Here Harriet first met the famous abolitionist Frederick Douglass.

After she was free, Harriet would do even more for the cause. She would write a book, speak to hundreds, join anti-slavery societies, and even take her services to the front lines of the Civil War. Harriet also became acquainted with Harriet Beecher Stowe, the

LINCOLN AND THE PIG

Later in his life, while riding with a group of men through a prairie, Lincoln passed a hog deeply mired in thick mud. The men passed by without giving much note. After moving on some distance, Lincoln stopped his horse. He told his companions that he could not stop thinking about the poor animal. He said that he imagined that it had said to itself, as the men passed by: "There now! my [sic] last hope is gone." Lincoln returned, crawled in the mud, dirtying himself sufficiently, and saved the poor creature.[32]

author of *Uncle Tom's Cabin,* arguably the most famous abolitionist book of the nineteenth century. After hearing Jacobs's story, Stowe proposed including it in the sequel to *Uncle Tom's Cabin.* She also gifted a signed copy of her famous book to Harriet Jacobs, something the Jacobs family would treasure for generations.[33]

Abolitionists such as Jacobs, Douglass, Stowe, and thousands of others had created a movement. The more they spoke, the more the American populace listened. The more America listened, the more apt they were to act, including Abraham Lincoln. This was the beginning of the end of slavery. In fact, it was reported by Stowe's son that when his mother met President Abraham Lincoln during the Civil War, he extended his hand and declared, "So you're the little woman who wrote the book that made this great war!"[34]

How was Lincoln prepared by these great abolitionists for his important role in ending slavery? In so many ways, his journey toward action against slavery is like that of many of us reading this book today. Like many of us, he was aware of the problem; indeed, he knew slavery existed in his day, just as most of us know it exists in our day. And, like most of us, he didn't approve. In fact, he highly disliked the practice.

But, like the vast majority of us today, Lincoln had never been a slave himself, nor had he been close to many

Frederick Douglass was perhaps the most influential African-American of the nineteenth century. After escaping slavery, he became a voice for the oppressed. He wrote eloquently and spoke passionately against the injustices of slavery and the oppression of other minorities. He was so effective that people began to listen. His goal was, as he stated, to "Agitate!, Agitate!, Agitate!" the American conscience.[35]

HARRIET BEECHER STOWE
AND HER BOOK

Years before the Civil War, a little-known, God-fearing woman left her home in Cincinnati one day and crossed the river to visit the neighboring state of Kentucky. Harriet Beecher Stowe would never be the same again. That day, she wandered onto a Kentucky plantation, and the true evil of human bondage set in. Slavery hit her between the eyes. She was horrified—not only at how the Southern states perpetuated this crime against God and man, but more so at how the Northern states did not care. She knew that taking no stance was, in fact, taking a stance.

After Harriet expressed her concerns to family members, her sister sent her a letter asking her to "write something that would make this whole nation feel what an accursed thing slavery is." Upon receiving and reading the letter, Harriet stood from her chair, crumpled the letter in her fisted hand, and declared, "I will write something. I will if I live!"[36] Harriet wrote *Uncle Tom's Cabin*, a fictional account of American slavery that told the truth about what was happening and shined a light upon the dark works of man. The book was published in 1852 and had sold more than a million copies within just a few years of its release. She had awakened the nation from its slumber.

people who were. And, as a politician who mostly represented people who were as disconnected from slavery as he was, it would have been natural and generally acceptable for him to sideline any policy proposals to abolish the practice. That was what all his predecessors to the presidency had done, and that was what the vast majority of white Americans had also done and were in fact still doing.

Perhaps that was why, even as he began his presidency, he didn't come in as an abolitionist by any stretch of the imagination. I don't mean to downplay Lincoln's true efforts and feelings against slavery as he entered the presidency. After all, he had just been elected as the first Republican president, and the Republican Party was largely founded on an anti-slavery platform. But only radical factions within the party were abolitionists who wanted direct action against the wicked practice. Lincoln was not part of that group. Though, again, he hated the practice and promised to fight to halt the expansion of slavery into new states and territories, he had no intention of attacking slavery where it existed in the South. He even promised during his First Inaugural Address: "I have no purpose, directly or indirectly, to interfere with the institution of slavery in the States where it exists. I believe I have no lawful right to do so, and I have no inclination to do so."[37] In the sense of taking direct action in the matter, Lincoln was not one of the original abolitionists.

But something happened to him. Something happened that needs to happen to all of us today. *A conversion.* Lincoln became converted to the idea that it was in fact his moral mandate to stand up, join the movement the abolitionists had created, and, using whatever tools he had at his disposal, destroy slavery in every part of the country where it reared its ugly head. Yes, he became a passionate abolitionist. So, how did he get there? By answering this question, perhaps we will learn something about how we can get there and become abolitionists *today.*

IN LINCOLN'S WORDS

"This declared indifference . . . for the spread of slavery, I cannot but hate. I hate it because of the monstrous injustice of slavery itself" (October 1854).[38]

"The Negro is a man [and] his bondage is cruelly wrong" (August 1855).[39]

"[The Declaration of Independence was the Founders'] majestic interpretation of the Universe. This was their lofty, and wise, and noble understanding of the justice of the Creator to His creatures. Yes, gentlemen, to all his creatures, to the whole great family of man. In their enlightened belief, nothing stamped with the Divine image and likeness was sent into the world to be trodden on, and degraded, and imbruted by its fellows" (August 1858).[40]

"I think slavery is wrong, morally and politically. I desire that it should be no further spread in these United States, and I should not object if it should gradually terminate in the whole Union" (September 1859).[41]

For Lincoln, his conversion to abolitionism largely grew out of events surrounding his election to the presidency. As a Republican who had voiced his opposition to the spread of slavery, he was instantly hated by the South. They feared this new president would come in and liberate their slaves. Southern states began to officially secede from the United States over this fear, even before Lincoln had arrived in Washington, D.C., to take his position. In order to persuade the South to come back to the Union, Lincoln promised he would not touch slavery, and he meant it (hence, his above-cited promise during his First Inaugural Address).

Instead of listening to or trusting Lincoln on the matter, the South instead doubled down. One by one, Southern states declared independence from the Union, then seized and/or launched military attacks on United States property in the South, including U.S. forts and ports. Those installations and entities did not belong to the Southern states; rather, they belonged to *all* the states, to *all* the people, to the *whole* Union. Lincoln and the rest of the nation in the North felt they were under attack. It was an internal invasion. So naturally they responded militarily, not to hit slavery, but to defend their national property in the South and restore the Union. This was the reason, and the only reason, Lincoln originally commanded that troops be sent into the South to engage in war. And this was the reason, the only reason, Northern soldiers obeyed. Most of them had never even met a black person, much less a slave. They didn't really care or think much about that evil thing called slavery that seemed so far away from them and their lives. They just wanted to preserve the United States.

But after a year of battling the South, the pressures of war, along with the persuasive voices of the abolitionists, made Lincoln reconsider everything. Remember, Lincoln was the boy who, after seeing chattel slavery for the first time, declared: "By God, boys,

"SOUTHERN INTENT"

Why did the South leave the Union and fight a bloody war to remain apart from it? The president and vice president of the Confederacy spoke frequently about the need for Southern victory in order to preserve slavery; they called slavery the "great truth," "the foundation," and the "cornerstone" of their new government.[42] Before the war, the would-be Confederate president, Jefferson Davis, "had frequently spoken to the United States Senate about the significance of slavery to the South and had threatened secession if what he perceived as Northern threats to the institution continued."[43] At the onset of the war, Confederate Vice President Alexander Stephens stated that slavery was "the proper status of the negro in our civilization" and that the issue of slavery was "the immediate cause of the late rupture and present revolution."[44]

In South Carolina's secession convention (the principal and most important secession convention), the delegates discussed their fears that Lincoln would allow "black Republicans" who were "hostile to slavery" to take positions of leadership in the government.[45] They could not have been any clearer than they were in their own document: the "Declaration of the Immediate Causes Which Induce and Justify the Secession of South Carolina from the Federal Union and their Ordinance of Secession." They printed it in black and white for all to read—their rebellion and secession was due to the "increasing hostility on the part of the non-slave-holding States to the Institution of Slavery."[46]

The Confederate constitution made Southern intent even clearer: "Our new Government is founded . . . upon the great truth that the negro is not the equal of the white man. That slavery—subordination to the superior race, is his natural and normal condition."[47] During the war, Confederate President Jefferson Davis sought to make slaves of all black people in America, even free ones. In response to the Emancipation Proclamation, Davis ordered the following: "On or after February 22, 1863, all free negroes within the limits of the Southern Confederacy shall be placed on slave status, and be deemed to be chattels, they and their issue forever." The order was to be executed even upon free black persons outside Confederate territory. Davis ordered that black people "taken in any of the States in which slavery does not now exist . . . shall be adjudged . . . to occupy the slave status." Said Davis, the black race is "an inferior race, peaceful and contented laborers in their sphere."[48]

Through the years and into the present day, Southern sympathizers have tried to make the argument that the South was not fighting for slavery as evidenced by the fact that relatively few Confederates actually owned slaves. These Southern apologists fail to comprehend a slave society. White Southerners saw their slaves as property, just as farmers today view their farm equipment—their tractors, their horses, their cattle. If all the farm equipment and livestock just disappeared in any agricultural economy, everyone would be affected, though relatively few actually own the equipment. Without these tools, the working folks (even those without the equipment) would have nothing to do, nowhere to go. The folks that buy and sell agricultural products (even those without farm equipment) would likewise find themselves jobless. They all want and need the farm owner to preserve his tools and equipment. Likewise, most Southerners (whether slave owners or not) wanted and needed their slavery. They understood what was at stake in this war. So should we.

Chandra Manning, a professor of history at Georgetown University, conducted a lengthy and in-depth study of Civil War letters, newspapers, and other primary source documents in order to determine why the South fought. "[It is] patronizing and insulting to Confederate soldiers," concluded Professor Manning, "to pretend they did not understand the war as a battle for slavery when they so plainly described it as exactly that."[49]

let's get away from this. If ever I get the chance to hit that thing, I'll hit it hard."[50] Was the war his *chance?* Could Lincoln come to see, as the abolitionists had already seen, that the Civil War was not, as Douglass taught, "a mere strife for territory and dominion, but a contest of civilization against barbarism"?[51]

As Lincoln continued pondering the question of slavery, something happened that, perhaps more than anything else, directed his thoughts and goals on the matter. It was a personal tragedy of great magnitude—the sudden death, by typhoid fever, of his eleven-year-old son, Willie.

As if it were not already the most difficult of times for Lincoln—losing a war he thought he would win fast, being hated on all sides, being questioned and betrayed by friends, and knowing his decision to stay in the war was leading to tens of thousands of deaths—on top of it all, he now had the ultimate parental nightmare thrown upon him.

Why Willie? On February 20, 1862, this was all the president could think as he looked upon the lifeless body of the boy. This was *his* boy. Of all his children, it was Willie who looked like Lincoln (tall and thin), who thought like Lincoln (pensive and analytical). Willie was his father's constant companion. Now what would he do? Upon the moment of Willie's death, Lincoln felt instantly lost. He stumbled into his secretary's office and declared, "My boy is gone—he is actually gone!" He then began to sob. When he later entered the room where Willie's body was laid after being washed and dressed, Lincoln stopped and looked at his child's face. He then "buried his head in his hands, and his tall frame was convulsed with emotion."[52] To make matters worse, after the boy's death, Mary Lincoln became inconsolable and would never recover.[53] The Lincolns had already lost their three-year-old Eddie a few years earlier. To ask them to also give up their Willie was unbearable. Upon looking at Willie's lifeless body, Lincoln exclaimed, "He was too good for this earth . . . but we loved him so."[54]

For weeks after the boy's death, Lincoln would just disappear every Thursday (the day Willie had died). He would go to the quiet, lonely room where Willie had passed away. He went to grieve, to meditate, and to weep in solitude.[55]

During these dark days, Lincoln was described by an eyewitness as a tormented soul, sleepless and pacing the halls of the White House, "his hands behind him, great black rings under his eyes, his head bent forward upon his breast,—altogether such a picture of the effects of sorrow, care, and anxiety as would have melted the hearts of the worst of his adversaries."[56] Journalist Noah Brooks was surprised to see how the once "happy-faced lawyer" had by 1862 become sad and stooped, with "a sunken deathly look about the large, cavernous eyes."[57] Lincoln would try, at times in vain, to self-medicate with his relentless storytelling and humor. But Lincoln admitted that "nothing could touch the tired spot within, which was all tired."[58]

As difficult as this was, perhaps it was a reflection of God's will at last being done. Sometimes heaven's medicine is not pleasant, but if it is given, it is necessary. It was precisely during these trying months that Lincoln, not knowing what else to do, turned to God like never before. As he would later admit: "I have been driven many times upon my knees by the overwhelming conviction that I had nowhere else to go."[59]

According to government printer John DeFrees, Lincoln (though always a God-fearing man) became much more of a religionist "about the time of the death of his son Willie," which had seemingly provoked in Lincoln a desire to expound and converse "on the subject of religion."[60] Mary Lincoln implied that as the war became increasingly intense, so did the president's reading of the Bible. In fact, several witnesses during this time commented on how they had stumbled in upon the president—whether in his office or in an obscure corner of a steamboat transport—"reading a dog-eared pocket copy of the New Testament." Lincoln's long-time friend Joshua Speed noted that, though Lincoln had been somewhat of a religious skeptic in his more youthful days, he had now "sought to become a believer."[61]

For Lincoln, empathy might have been the most valuable thing he gained. His personal pain made the pain of slavery too difficult to ignore. And his reading and pondering over biblical principles likely compounded the pressure on him to feel more and do more to bring relief to those struggling in bondage.

As president, Lincoln had immense power. He commanded armies. And those armies were fighting in the Southern states, where slavery existed. Might he find a way to now use those armies not only to preserve the Union but also to attack slavery? The voices of the abolitionists rang loud and clear.

Lincoln knew if he began discussing the possibility of emancipation, his friends, his cabinet, and the entire country would be deeply concerned. He had promised the nation he would not touch slavery, except to limit its expansion into new states and territories. If he were to now start freeing slaves, he

IN HARRIET'S WORDS

"The memory of the past in my early life, the cruel wrongs that a slave must suffer, has served to bind me more closely to those around me; whatever I have done or may do, is a [C]hristian duty I owe to my race—I owe it to God's suffering poor. When these grateful creatures gather around me, some looking so sad and desolate, while others with their faces beaming happiness, and their condition so much improved by the blessings of freedom, I can but feel within my heart the last chain is to be broken, the accursed blot wiped out. This lightens my labours, and if any sacrifices have been made, they are forgotten."[62]

might lose the support of his Union troops, especially from the border slave states (like Maryland) that protected slavery while still being loyal to the Union.

Again, the war wasn't meant to be about eradicating slavery where it already existed. But times had changed—Lincoln had changed—and he felt he needed to drastically alter course. But he knew these were dangerous thoughts, so he mostly kept them to himself and to God. He openly declared, "I talk to God," and admitted the following to General Dan Sickles: "When I could not see any other resort, I would place my whole reliance in God, knowing that all would be well, and that He would decide for the right."[63]

"It has pleased Almighty God to put me in my present position," Lincoln told one friend in the spring of 1862, "and looking up to him for divine guidance, I must work out my destiny as best I can."[64]

When the subject of emancipating slaves came up, he would simply say that "it is my earnest desire to know the will of Providence in this matter. And if I can learn what it is I will do it."[65] In the fall of 1862, Lincoln admitted that the subject of emancipating slaves was "on my mind, by day and by night, more than any other. Whatever shall appear to be God's will, I will do."[66]

During those dark and confusing months of 1862, a friend and Baptist minister, Noyes Miner, told Lincoln that "Christian people all over the country are praying for you as they never prayed for a mortal man before," to which Lincoln responded: "This is an encouraging thought to me. If I were not sustained by the prayers of God's people I could not endure this constant pressure."[67]

The events leading up to and through 1862 ultimately provided what Lincoln sought. Revelations began arriving, and his conversion began solidifying. Lincoln described it as "a process of crystallization" during which he "constantly prayed."[68]

POWERFUL VOICES AGAINST SLAVERY

Frederick Douglass: "It is not light that is needed, but fire; it is not the gentle shower, but thunder. We need the storm, the whirlwind, and the earthquake. The feeling of the nation must be quickened; the conscience of the nation must be roused; the propriety of the nation must be startled; the hypocrisy of the nation must be exposed; and its crimes against God and man must be proclaimed and denounced. . . . The American people and the Government at Washington may refuse to recognize it for a time; but the inexorable logic of events will force it upon them in the end; that the war now being waged in this land is a war for and against slavery."[69]

Harriet Jacobs (during the second year of the Civil War): "Our prayers and tears have gone up as a memorial of our wrongs before him who created us—and who will judge us—Man may desire to stand still but an arm they cannot repel is leading them on. . . . A just God is settling the account."[70]

John Jacobs (Harriet's brother): "You that have believed in the promise, and obeyed His word, are beginning to see the moving of His hand to execute judgment and bestow mercy. Those who have long sown chains and fetters will reap blood and carnage."[71]

Harriet Beecher Stowe: "Not surer is the eternal law by which the millstone sinks into the ocean, than that stronger law by which injustice and cruelty shall bring on nations the wrath of Almighty God."[72]

And then he said it out loud: *I think I should free the slaves.* He quietly told his best friend in the cabinet, Secretary of State William Seward. It was during the summer of 1862 while they rode together in a carriage on their way to a funeral. The funeral was for the small child of Secretary of War Edwin Stanton.[73] Perhaps this event reminded Lincoln of Willie and caused him to feel again the deep empathy his own boy's death had instilled in him. He knew he could trust Seward and reveal to him what was on his mind, though it seems he was not completely sure about the decision yet. But the answer was becoming clearer.

Seward's response was a wise one: he told Lincoln to wait for a Union military victory. Otherwise, he said, with the Union army experiencing defeat after defeat, an Emancipation Proclamation would seem like a "last measure of an exhausted government, . . . our last shriek, on the retreat."[74] Lincoln did as his friend suggested—and what followed was one of the great miracles of American history.

A few months passed, and summer had turned to fall. It was now September 1862—about six months since Willie had died—and Lincoln was done waiting. He took up pen and paper and wrote something almost unbelievable: "In the present civil war, it is quite possible that God's purpose is something different from the purpose of either party. . . . I am almost ready to say this is probably true—that *God wills this contest,* and wills that it shall not end yet."[75] Throughout the history of the world, what commander-in-chief would dare say such a thing? Yes, it is easy to argue that your enemy is wrong; but to suggest that your own side is also wrong? To suggest that God is doing this awful thing to both sides for some purpose heretofore unknown? It was like something out of the biblical account of ancient Israel.

Of course, he was not about to share this message with anyone.

He would have sounded like he was morphing into a prophet—not a safe move for the president of the United States. And so he tucked the memo away; it was, after all, not intended for anyone to see. In fact, it would not be discovered among the Lincoln papers for years. When Lincoln's secretary happened upon it one day, he was moved. He later explained that the note was "not written to be seen of men. It was penned in the awful sincerity of a perfectly honest soul trying to bring itself into closer communion with its maker."[76]

Having hid the memo—which was titled "Meditation on the Divine Will"—Lincoln found himself again on his knees. Reports were coming in: a fierce battle (what would be the famous Battle of Antietam) was looming large. Lincoln knew he had been very clear to the nation the previous year during his First Inaugural Address—*I will not touch slavery in the South* was the take-home message. Lincoln now recognized he had been wrong. The nation had been mired in the sin of slavery for too long. Now God was purging the land—both North and South—of the iniquity. Lincoln was trying to get in line with "the Divine Will."

As he prayed during the days and hours before that September battle, one thought prevailed above the others. Lincoln later testified to his colleagues that, at that moment, he "had made a vow, a covenant, that if God gave us victory in the approaching battle, he would consider it an indication of the Divine Will, and that it was his duty to move forward in the cause of emancipation."[77] This was the battle he was waiting for.

If Lincoln was expecting divine intervention, then the miraculous events directly contributing to Union victory at Antietam did not disappoint.

While Lincoln was on his knees making a covenant with God, seeking light in the darkness of war, and hoping the pending battle would provide what he needed to proceed with emancipating slaves, something very interesting was happening to a certain Union soldier.

His name was Corporal Barton Mitchell, and he was as common as any other private in the Union army. Mitchell, along with Union forces, had recently descended upon Frederick, Maryland, some thirty miles from the site of Antietam, where the battle was just days away from rocking the land. While Mitchell was walking through a field outside of town (likely near to where his unit had made camp), he stumbled upon something incredible.

Days before Corporal Mitchell found himself in this field, Confederate General Robert E. Lee had convened a war council near that very spot. During the meeting, Lee announced a daring plan that would culminate in the Battle of Antietam. If his secret plan could be executed correctly, he would score his first real victory in Northern territory, and nothing would then stop him from marching into Washington, D.C. His secret plan called for his army to divide into several parts, then converge upon the Northern troops. The plan was extremely risky because it would leave several Confederate divisions isolated and exposed. And so, extreme care was taken to account for the few written copies of the plan, which Lee called Special Order #191. Lee insisted that the copies remain secured.

Having left that field to execute their daring plan, no Confederate officer at that secret meeting would ever be able to explain what happened days later to Union Corporal Mitchell in that field. In fact, up until the present day, *nobody* has been able to fully explain it. For the thing Mitchell randomly stumbled upon in that field was an envelope wrapped around three cigars. Pulling the envelope off of the cigars, Corporal Mitchell opened it and read the profound message—a copy of Lee's Special Order #191.

Mitchell knew what he needed to do. The battle plans were

immediately sent up the chain of command. Before long, they found their way into the hands of the Union commander, General George McClellan. Then, in a second miracle, McClellan was able to immediately verify the order's authenticity because his aide had been close friends in the pre-war U.S. Army with Lee's adjutant, Robert Chilton. The Union aide quickly recognized his old Southern friend's handwriting. "Here is a paper," McClellan then declared, "with which if I cannot whip 'Bobbie Lee,' I will be willing to go home."[78]

Thanks in part to the miraculously delivered military intelligence, the Union pulled off a narrow victory at Antietam. In such a close battle, which could have gone either way, that piece of intelligence almost certainly tipped the scales (though most military historians agree that McClellan did not take full advantage of the miraculous intelligence). Had the North lost the battle, the South would have been in a perfect position. They would have defeated the Union in its own territory. The entire war could have then quickly ended in favor of the South, and its prize would have been the perpetual existence

DOUGLASS ON LINCOLN

"His great mission was to accomplish two things: first, to save his country from dismemberment and ruin; and second, to free his country from the great crime of slavery. To do one or the other, or both, he must have the earnest sympathy and the powerful cooperation of his loyal fellow countrymen. Without this primary and essential condition to success his efforts must have been vain and utterly fruitless. Had he put the abolition of slavery before the salvation of the Union, he would have inevitably driven from him a powerful class of American people and rendered resistance to rebellion impossible. Viewed from the genuine abolition ground, Mr. Lincoln seemed tardy, cold, dull, and indifferent; measuring him by the sentiment of his country, a sentiment he was bound as a statesmen to consult, he was swift, zealous, radical and determined."[79]

of human captivity.[80] The Union cause was miraculously saved! The Pulitzer Prize–winning historian and renowned expert on Antietam, James McPherson, concluded that "the odds against the sequence of events that led to the loss and finding and verification of these orders must have been a million to one."[81]

Days after the news of the Union victory at Antietam arrived at the capital, Lincoln called an emergency cabinet meeting. He knew what he now needed to do. He had covenanted with God, and God had responded. It was September 22, 1862. The president marched into that meeting and boldly declared that "his mind was fixed, his decision made." It was clear to all present that any objection to his call for emancipation would be immediately dismissed. The president told his cabinet not to bother him over "the main matter—for I have determined for myself."[82] He then laid upon the table a sacred document: the preliminary draft of the Emancipation Proclamation.

In an emotional state, Lincoln then declared unequivocally that "God had decided this question in favor of the slaves." The president continued: "I will keep the promise to myself, and"—he paused here for emphasis—"to my maker."[84] The secretary of the navy took notes on what he had witnessed during this cabinet meeting. He wrote that Lincoln had, at that moment, made a "covenant" with the Almighty.[85] Referring to Lincoln's newfound belief that emancipation was the *real* purpose of the war, one

CONFRONTED BY HIS WIFE

After Lincoln had made his decision on emancipation, even his own wife questioned this profound change from his early policies and promises. She asked, *Will you really go through with it?* With a glance to heaven, then back to Mary, he simply replied: "I am a man under orders; I cannot do otherwise."[83]

prominent historian stated, "Truly, it was a 'Damascus Road' experience for the president."[86]

Shortly after the Emancipation Proclamation was issued, Harriet Jacobs attended a meeting hosted by the New England Anti-Slavery Society. Along with her many other abolitionist efforts to liberate the captive, Harriet had been working to extract orphans caught in the violence of war and to find them homes in the North. Harriet was invited to speak at the conference about her adoption efforts. While at the meeting, Harriet also witnessed as the Society officially recognized that their hard work was paying off. They recognized that Lincoln had at last changed the national war agenda from "UNION" to "EMANCIPATION AND UNION." Though the fight was not over yet, the country was at last on the right path.[87]

◆ ◆ ◆

So many applicable lessons can be learned from Lincoln's experience. The relevance of these applications lies in the perhaps counterintuitive idea that the abolishment of slavery in Lincoln's day did not result in the end of actual slavery. As Kevin Bales, professor of Contemporary Slavery, pointed out, the "abolition of slavery was immensely significant when laws were effectively enforced, but it also blinded people to ongoing slavery. Subsequent generations have been unaware that legal abolition didn't make slavery go away, that it only masked the problem. Behind closed doors, in remote places and right under our noses, slavery has continued, making people rich, feeding our lifestyles, and burning up lives."[88]

And so, in many ways, our mission to eradicate human bondage today is as real as was Lincoln's. Furthermore, while the nineteenth-century form of slavery differed in significant ways from modern-day slavery, the parallels are still stunningly informative.

PUSHING THE LIMITS: LINCOLN'S INGENIOUS PROCLAMATION

The truth born of his personal empathy for human suffering, along with military necessity, compelled Lincoln to look outside the box, get creative, and push the limits in order to do right. Lincoln realized, as he stated in his First Inaugural Address, that a president of the United States doesn't usually have the authority to free slaves. But he had searched and found a legal way to do it now. He explained that the Constitution allows a president during wartime to confiscate property of the enemy, especially when that property is being used to fight against the United States. Since the Southerners believed their slaves to be property, and used that property to support their war efforts, Lincoln used their wicked reasoning against them and decided he could free slaves ("confiscate enemy property") as a war power given to the president.

Even today, however, critics of Lincoln downplay his efforts, claiming that the Emancipation Proclamation did very little. They argue that, by staying within constitutional bounds, Lincoln was limiting himself to only freeing slaves in enemy territory where he had no power to free slaves, while the slaves in Union territory, where he actually had power to act, were left in chains.

Without the Proclamation, however, Union soldiers might have continued occupying Southern states, but they would have left slavery alone in those states. For example, early in the conflict, local emancipation orders by Union Generals Fremont and Hunter were rescinded.[89] They had been commanded to continue to retake the South, but to free no slaves. And so, yes, the Proclamation was necessary. Slavery was going nowhere without it.

With the Proclamation, however, once the South was conquered, the slaves were freed; and thus, the Proclamation did accomplish much. For critics to say (as they do) that the Proclamation did nothing is like saying the U.S. declarations of war against Imperial Japan and Nazi Germany did nothing because, initially, they were just declarations. Upon their issuance, Imperial Japan and Nazi Germany remained a force largely untouched by America. We need not add the obvious fact that these declarations eventually led the U.S. to defeat these foreign enemies. So it was with the Proclamation.

"The old cliché," wrote Civil War expert James McPherson, "that the proclamation did not free a single slave because it applied only to the Confederate states where Lincoln had no power, completely misses the point. The proclamation announced a revolutionary new war aim—the overthrow of slavery by force of arms if and when Union forces conquered the South."[90]

Lincoln's move was ingenious in other ways as well. By keeping the Proclamation within the bounds of the Constitution, his power to begin emancipation efforts remained safe from the often racist and often pro-South Supreme Court, who otherwise might have sought any legal justification to throw out the Proclamation the moment it was issued. But now the Court could do nothing. In the meantime, Lincoln would begin phase two of his emancipation plan: the Thirteenth Amendment, which would free the rest of the slaves in the country by constitutional mandate. Whereas the Proclamation was merely an executive order that could be overthrown by the Court, especially once the war ended—once Lincoln's legal excuse for freeing slaves ended—this new constitutional amendment would put the full, nationwide abolition of slavery beyond the misguided grasp of any person, officer, or judge in the land.

In light of the profound experiences that led him to issue the Proclamation, and in light of the inspired strategy he now employed, it is no wonder Lincoln concluded the Emancipation Proclamation by stating, "I invoke the considerate judgment of mankind, and the gracious favor of Almighty God."[91]

I have heard many students of history wonder out loud how it was that good people in America turned a blind eye to slavery for so long. *I would have been an abolitionist,* they declare, *if only I had been around then!* The problem with this line of thinking, though sincere, is that it is generally incorrect. Why? Because, for the most part, if somebody was willing to be an abolitionist in Lincoln's day, they most likely would already be one now. Think about this: Most people living in the Northern states, while aware of slavery, had never seen it. In fact, most of them probably didn't know or perhaps had never even met a black person. Indeed, these good Americans didn't travel to South Carolina or Georgia with any more frequency than Americans today travel to Haiti, or Southeast Asia, or other countries with high human trafficking rates. (Not that one needs to travel outside of the United States to see human trafficking, as there are tens of thousands of trafficking cases happening right here and right now in our own country.) And so, it was as easy for them to ignore as it is for us.

I recognize that I say this at the risk of sounding preachy, accusatory, and self-righteous. But that is not my intent at all. In fact, I have pointed out that I myself didn't run into the anti-trafficking effort with my sword unsheathed. Rather, I hid from it as long as I could. Really, I was pushed into it and basically forced to look. So I truly understand why there aren't more abolitionists today. As in Lincoln's day, people just don't know—and it's such a tough theme to address that people aren't necessarily running around trying to check into it.

My point is this: because we find ourselves today in a situation similar to that in which Lincoln and the North found themselves, we must each become converted, as Lincoln did. It wasn't immediate for him, and it won't be immediate for us, but we can learn from him how to become truly converted to the cause of human liberty.

In Lincoln's case, the first thing he did was educate himself on the issue. And, perhaps more important, he opened his heart to it. His personal grief and experiences helped him to do this. As award-winning Lincoln biographer Richard Carwardine explains, "Lincoln's private understanding of his moral obligations, and of the meaning of the conflict itself, evolved under the grueling burden of leadership, the wider suffering of wartime, and personal grief. . . . There is every sign that his understanding of providential intervention both shaped the thinking by which he reached the most profound of his decisions, for emancipation, and—even more powerfully—steeled his nerve to stand by the implications of that decision once made."[92]

We need to do the same. Though it hurts, we need to make slavery personal. We need to feel it. We need to imagine that these child victims are our own children. Then we will gain the empathy that will produce the courage to enter the fray and stay in it.

Lincoln also made his actions a matter of prayer. He turned to heaven for strength, wisdom, and guidance—and he asked and hoped for miracles. (Harriet Jacobs, of course, regularly did the same.) And then (also like Harriet), Lincoln got creative. He took what tools were at his disposal, and he outsmarted evil and did much to conquer it.

Nineteenth-century slavery was not eradicated because one day, after hundreds of years of human bondage, the president and/or the congress of the United States finally stood up and said, "At last it's over." Rather, it was the people—it was the masses who at last rose up. It was Frederick Douglass with his oration. It was Harriet Beecher Stowe with her book. It was the abolitionists and their sermons and their publications. The movement got so big that the government had to act and join along with it. This was the beginning of the end of historical slavery. And similar movements will prove to be the beginning of the end of modern-day slavery.

WHAT CAN I DO?

People ask me all the time, What can I do to help trafficked kids? And I always tell them the same thing: You will know the answer to that before I do. Each of us has a unique skill set. Each of us should, like Lincoln, get creative in how we contribute to the solution. Some are great writers, like Harriet Beecher Stowe. Others are great speakers, like Frederick Douglass. Some enjoy advocating for public policy, or fundraising, or putting on events. All of these things help. And, of course, O.U.R. is just one of many groups working toward a solution. We encourage people to support any of the groups here listed, as well as others they may come across.

Polaris Project
International Justice Mission
The National Center on Sexual Exploitation
The National Center for Missing and Exploited Children
ECPAT (End Child Prostitution and Trafficking)
Shared Hope International
Coalition of Immokalee Workers
Love 146
3Strands
Fight the New Drug

And then, if nothing else, just open your mouth. Talk about human trafficking. Tweet about it. Post articles and videos about it. Everytime I come home from a rescue operation, having seen once again the profundity of the plague of trafficking, I always become dumbfounded when I check my social media or online news feed. All of this media content seems so insignificant compared to the tragedy I just witnessed. The problem is so grave and so pervasive, it becomes shocking to me that modern-day slavery isn't the headline of every news outlet every day. It should be until we end it. Not enough people know about it. Not enough people are talking about it. You can help change that.

William Still

One of my heroes of the Underground Railroad was a man named William Still (1821-1902). Still was a free black man who lived in Philadelphia and worked as a businessman, philanthropist, and civil rights advocate. An operator along the Underground Railroad, Still documented hundreds of stories of slavery and slave escapes. His efforts were so important that some have called him the "Father of the Underground Railroad." Today, as historians piece together the story of American slavery, and how it was fought and defied, they almost certainly consult Still's book, *The Underground Railroad.* I personally have studied his publication to help me in my mission. Thank goodness he opened his mouth and took out his pen.

Your words today can be powerful as a means to liberate the captive, just as his were then. Remember the powerful statement often attributed to British statesman Edmund Burke: "The only thing necessary for the triumph of evil is for good men to do nothing."

CHAPTER 12

LITTLE MIA

The photos of Mia and Marky in my office include one taken by one of my undercover operators while the kids sat with me in the van, driving from the false orphanage to the hotel to execute the sting operation that would liberate them and their twenty-six little companions. Before, I had somewhat selfishly seen these pictures as O.U.R. coming to the rescue. I thought it was a depiction of me doing something for them. But I was wrong. It was actually them doing something for me.

When we discovered the whereabouts of Mia and Marky after having lost their location for about eight months, from there, our bond only grew. My wife and kids now know them well. We have spent countless hours with them. They have become our family. In this process, I have learned some important lessons, mostly through little Mia.

You can learn a lot from a child who was raised in slavery—especially one like Mia, who as a small child had become the primary caregiver to a baby, Marky. I cannot imagine a darker existence. First, the earthquake took almost everything from her. Then, traffickers sought to destroy the little she had left. How can a person (especially a child) conquer such darkness? How does one heal from this?

The answers to these questions are valuable beyond measure, for don't we all face darkness of some kind? Betrayal. Loss of loved ones. Sickness. Loneliness. Separation. Hate. Prejudice. Social injustice. The list is endless. Indeed, darkness surrounds us all. Don't we all need, plead, and pray for the light that will carry us out? Well, Mia found it!

I first began to *really* recognize this light in Mia when I came to visit her one day at her new orphanage, where she lived with Marky and approximately twenty other small children. I hadn't been there in a few months, so when I entered the gate and stepped into the courtyard, she and Marky ran to me and jumped into my arms, declaring as they always do: "Papa Blanc! Papa Blanc!" Shortly after greeting me, they grabbed my backpack and dug in to see what treasures they might find. It didn't take Mia long to pull out my box of chocolate protein bars. By the time I realized what was happening, Mia was running into the orphanage house with a huge smile on her face, holding the box of bars like a football. That box represented a few of the only meals I had for my team that week (we were about to head into the bush that day to check into some trafficking organizations). Notwithstanding, her spritely little spirit and the smile on her face as she ran away made me happy anyway. And I let her go.

A few minutes later, Mia came out of the house. The box was in her hand still. As she came to the cement floor of the courtyard where I stood, she stopped and looked at me. Her smile was as bright as before—maybe even brighter now. She then turned the box upside down, showing me that all the contents had disappeared. She couldn't hold back a mischievous little giggle.

Our director of aftercare happened to be with me and watched the scene curiously. "Oh, no, Tim," she said. "Mia may be a hoarder."

"What do you mean?" I asked.

"Well," said the director, "hoarding is a common condition

for kids who have spent a time in their lives not knowing when their next meal would come. Even when there is an abundance of food, sometimes they will still take what they can and hide it away, just in case."

I understood. And knowing what I did about Mia's past, it made perfect sense.

"Mia," I said calmly as I approached the still smiling little girl, "show me where the chocolate bars are, okay?"

Mia grabbed my hand and practically dragged me into the house. After my director's warning, I had half expected that Mia would show me some grotesque nest of maggot-infested food piled up in a corner with fresh chocolate protein bars poking out of its sides. But her excitement told me that perhaps I was in store for something completely different.

"See, Papa Blanc!" she said as we approached a door inside the home. "Look!" she said as she then pushed open the door. There before me in the small room, ten little children about four to six years old sat around a table. They had apparently been do-ing some sort of coloring book school project, but they were all taking a break. Someone had given them what they thought were chocolate bars (really, my protein bars), and they were all gnawing away at the harder-to-bite-into-than-expected bars as best they could. I couldn't help but laugh out loud.

But my laugh quickly turned to tears of tenderness and joy as I watched what Mia did next.

"Papa Blanc!" she said. "Please, we need one more bar. Little Pierre did not get one." She pointed to a small boy sitting at the table with nothing to gnaw on. "I ran out of chocolate, Papa Blanc! Please get just one more!"

I looked down at her hands. No chocolate bar. I looked at her pockets. No bar. I quickly counted the children with chocolate against the number of bars advertised on the box. My hunch was right on. She had given them *all* away, saving nothing for herself. And here she was now, still thinking not of herself but only of little Pierre; she was asking for only one more bar, not two.

About six months later, I was back at the orphanage. I had come to see the kids for Christmas and give them presents from home. I first brought out an enormous duffel bag with enough toys for every child in the orphanage. Mia was first in line as I opened the bag—but, again, not for the reason you might think. She dug into that bag for one reason only: to find the perfect toy for each and every one of her classmates. When the bag was empty, she looked around at all her friends. She smiled at their joy. Again, she kept *nothing* for herself and wanted nothing. Her joy was full in serving the others.

I had thought this might happen. That was why I had brought another bag with me, full of special gifts just for her. I took the bag out, opened it, and called Mia over to me.

"Mia," I said, "you are the kindest child I have ever met. You love your friends, don't you?"

She smiled shyly and nodded her head.

"Well," I continued, "these gifts here are for you. My kids at home bought them for you, and you *must* keep them."

She just looked at me. Her eyes glistened, full of hope and charity.

"Do you understand?" I asked her.

She smiled and nodded again.

She then dropped to her knees and began to rummage through the different gifts in the bag. She looked at and handled each toy, intermittently eyeing her classmates, who were already busy playing with the toys they had been given. All the while she periodically glanced up at me to see if I were still paying attention. I couldn't believe what I perceived she was thinking about doing. I had never seen a child do this. *Ever.* Of course, this *was* the child who, while in a state of starvation and being held by traffickers, gave up half her candy bar to her baby brother without thinking twice. That had been my first encounter with her. Why should this be any different?

I decided not to intervene. I stepped back and pretended to be focusing on something else. So long as she thought I was watching, she might not take her natural course.

Once I had her convinced that I was completely distracted, I watched out of the corner of my eye as she dragged the duffel bag near to where the other kids were playing. She then carefully distributed each and every toy to her little orphan friends.

She can't help herself! I thought to myself. Right then and there I gave her a nickname—a most oxymoronic nickname: "the mischievous giver." I was dumbfounded.

Mia did keep one gift that day, a book my youngest child at home had bought for her: *Oh, the Places You'll Go,* by Dr. Seuss. After delivering the last of her toys to her friends, she walked over to a bench in the corner of the courtyard and opened the book. I watched from a distance as she just stared at the first page, never turning it. As I walked over and sat by her, I instantly realized why she hadn't turned the page. In the front of the book, my wife had pasted our brand-new family Christmas card. It was the reason she hadn't given up this one gift. Mia then began to point to each of my children in the picture, as she always loved to do, repeating each of their names to me. I put my arm around her, and she nestled her head into my side.

"I love you, Papa Blanc," she said. I tried to reply, but, overcome with emotion, I couldn't get the words out. I just hugged her tighter. I had never been so close to such a powerful little light in all my life.

◆ ◆ ◆

As I stood in my office, lost in thought, gazing at the sweet pictures of Mia and Marky, it hit me again: *Mia has learned the secret!* In the darkness of the trenches of her personal war, she learned how to turn the lights on. *Service!* It occurred to me that we adults think we have it figured out. We think that the more we have, the happier we are. Sure, we'll give a little of our time and resources here and there, but the bulk we will keep. How fooled we are!

This child, who probably couldn't even articulate with words what she was doing, had figured out the formula that I never could have discovered on my own. Her unique, lived experience had taught her profound truth, and now she was passing this truth on to me. She needed to get herself and her baby brother out of severe darkness and pain, and so she figured it out. She figured out how to find light. *Light* comes through serving others. *Happiness* comes through serving others. *Healing* comes through serving others.

THE MAGIC OF SERVICE

"Everybody can be great . . . because anybody can serve. You don't have to have a college degree to serve. You don't have to make your subject and verb agree to serve. You only need a heart full of grace. A soul generated by love."[93]

—*Martin Luther King Jr.*

CHAPTER 13

GUESNO MARDY

s I turned from the pictures of Mia and Marky, I walked over
to the photograph of Guesno Mardy. It was the same lesson.
It was the same truth.

The picture, which sits next to the portrait of Harriet
Tubman, was one we had taken after a particularly powerful day
of planning a series of rescue operations in Haiti. You may ask
why Guesno, this churchman and orphanage director, would
have been involved in rescue operations. The answer to that query
is the lesson I was learning yet again.

You will recall that the last time we discussed Guesno in
this book, he had just learned that his son Gardy was not found
among the trafficked children at the false orphanage. Guesno responded by saying he was willing to take on the sacrifice, to let
his son go, if that meant that the others could be rescued. He
then brought eight of those rescued children home to care for
them as if they were his own children.

I recognized in that moment the powerful light that was in
Guesno. I recognized then that his service and sacrifice for others was what kept that light burning. I had recognized the same
pattern before in Mia and others. But perhaps I had not fully
internalized it or let it sink in until now. After discussing it all
with Coach Tomlin and hearing out Burgess—after connect-
ing the entire story to Harriet Tubman and the Underground

Railroad—only now was it all falling into place. Only now was I *really* comprehending Guesno.

When Harriet Tubman escaped slavery, something happened to her. "When I found I had crossed that line," she later recalled, "I looked at my hands to see if I was the same person. There was such a glory over everything; the sun came like gold through the trees, and over the fields, and I felt like I was in Heaven." She knew she was blessed, though her people and her country still lived in darkness. But she knew the light and would work for the rest of her life to magnify and to share that light. Even if it meant risking everything, including her freedom and her own life, she would go farther, work harder, dig deeper in the service of others.

Guesno had experienced something similar. He was surrounded by darkness. Death, loss, mayhem, and slavery were all around him. But he had also known the light. His wife and other children had been spared in the earthquake. He still had them. His faith in God continued. He still had that. And he had his freedom. Indeed, he was still free to act. And so, instead of cursing God and dying, he, like Tubman, chose to take the freedom and light he had and magnify it in the service of others. As with Mia, service became his balm of Gilead. The more he employed it, the more the light came, and the more he healed from his incomprehensible wounds.

"Tim," he asked me shortly after the Mia and Marky rescue mission, "when is our next rescue?"

I didn't know what to tell him at first. Certainly he had done enough. I couldn't fully comprehend at the time why he would want to give more—or risk more. But I knew I couldn't tell this man no. So I paired him up with a top O.U.R. operator, a Haitian-American we will call Darius. Darius has served both in the U.S. Army and later for the Haitian police (he maintains duel citizenship). His story and sacrifice to liberate the captive is beyond inspiring. But, for security reasons, it must go untold for now. Like Tubman, Darius and Guesno do not serve to be seen of men. They serve because they love.

Darius and Guesno have since led multiple operations in some of the most dangerous places on the planet. Due to his business and government connections and spotless reputation, Guesno has led out as a liaison officer for O.U.R., while Darius focuses on the operations and training side. Although most of their efforts can't be discussed, there is one case I can highlight, with permission of the Haitian government.

It began with a tip to Darius—kids were being trafficked for sex in the backrooms of night clubs and brothels in various locations around Port-au-Prince. With the authorization and top cover of the Haitian National Police, Darius called a group of O.U.R. undercover operators to play the role of American sex tourists in order to infiltrate this black market. The team quickly got in with the trafficking heads, and, after several weeks, were brought into the dark. The operators helped the police identify more than two dozen victims, including children as young as ten or eleven years old, who were being used for sex and also as the subjects of child rape videos that had been produced and then distributed internationally.

The prime target in the case, the Haitian kingpin of child trafficking, was a woman by the name of Franciane Dorlus. But she was known on the streets as "Cho" (translation, "Hot"), which in her culture had sexual connotations.

Cho was as wicked as she was elusive. Unlike other brothels in town that were brick-and-mortar buildings, easy to identify as nightclubs or brothels, Cho's criminal enterprise tended to be hidden and spread out. Steel doors in various parts of town lined the streets, appearing to the common passerby to be closed-down shops. In fact, these doors were the gateways to the nightmarish existence of Cho's and her criminal colleagues' victims.

I will never forget receiving the first reports from our undercover operators who had, after weeks of dangerous work, become chummy with Cho and the other traffickers. Convinced they were nothing more than wealthy American pedophiles, Cho at last opened one of these doors and let my operators in. The door opened to a dark cement hallway with metal planks hanging on the walls by chains. Cho explained that the girls sat on these planks, waiting to be gawked at, chosen, and finally purchased. At the end of the hallway was a small room with a bed—the destination every girl prayed would not be hers, but always was.

Cho asked if the American men would like her to bring out some of the girls, who were apparently being showcased in other dark hallways. Our operators, acting as though they were still scared of being caught by authorities, told her no. Instead, they offered up another arrangement.

You see, the police, along with our operators, were intentionally not pushing hard to see the girls immediately, which would have then activated a raid and arrest. If one trafficking ring went down before we got to all the others, then those others would run and hide, making it nearly impossible to find them and rescue their victims. Also, we had not obtained enough evidence as of yet to ensure a prosecution would stick on Cho, even if she had brought the girls out on display. We needed to work a little harder.

The designed plan of the Haitian police was this: We would organize a large "sex party" at a beach resort (one of the few holdovers remaining in Haiti from its days as a resort destination). The beach would be filled with Americans there for a party, which would provide the excuse needed for Cho and the traffickers to work together, pool their resources, and bring *all* their victims. Only then could we liberate them *all*. The police asked O.U.R. to provide these "American partyers." Tapping into our large network of contractors (former U.S. and Australian military, police, and intelligence personnel), we were ready to fill the beach and set the trap.

We needed the traffickers to feel that the party—and more important, the partygoers—were legit. In order to help convince them, O.U.R. used a beautiful yacht that a friend had lent us for this operation. When the traffickers saw that the Americans had traveled in on this yacht, they would know this was no Haitian police operation. Also, the party was planned for Super Bowl Sunday—a day the traffickers knew Americans would naturally gather together and party hard. (How the NFL keeps entering this story in the most unique ways remains a mystery to me. Perhaps, in part, it has something to do with the fact that Super Bowl day, with its massive party emphasis, is considered by some experts to be the largest single trafficking day in the year.)

Thanks to the selfless, behind-the-scenes work of Guesno, Darius, the brave Haitian officers, and O.U.R. operators, everything had run like clockwork. Everything was set—except for the one thing we feared but could not control: the corruption that was famous in Haiti. These were powerful traffickers. After their arrests, what would stop them from finding willing judges and buying their way out of jail?

"I can't guarantee that won't happen, Tim," was the response from Joseph Guerson, the lead Haitian detective in the case. He was a good man, and one we had vetted using outside sources. He was also the same detective who had led the Mia and Marky rescue operation years earlier.

Tim Ballard and Officer Joseph Guerson during an undercover operation

"I wish I could tell you it won't happen," he continued, "but it's impossible to know if some judge will be convinced to break the law after this all goes down. It's a real possibility."

There was still time to cancel the operation. Many agencies and organizations had advised us not to work in Haiti for this very reason, and we had weighed out every option going into this. I sat down with Guesno one last time before giving the final green light for O.U.R. to participate and risk attaching its name and reputation to a mission that could fail in the aftermath for reasons beyond our control.

"Please don't quit on this, Tim. I beg you." I looked into Guesno's eyes. He loved his country, problematic as it was. He loved his son. And the kids we would rescue—including the countless kids who would never be taken in the future because their would-be captors would be locked up—were a reflection of his son. Guesno knew that success followed success. The more we could operate successfully in Haiti, the better chance we would have to eventually rescue Gardy. Giving up now, notwithstanding the challenges before us, would be to give up on Gardy and thousands of others.

"Besides," he reasoned, "even if they get out, at least something will have happened. At least they will think twice about the evil they are doing. The country will know. The press will know. No matter what, something good will come of it." I marveled at Guesno's passion as he pled with me.

"And what's the alternative, Tim?" Guesno grabbed my hands tightly in his. "Think about it! What's the alternative? Do nothing? Then what will happen? I'll tell you what will happen. Just that: *Nothing!* Kids will just keep getting hurt. Traffickers will continue to grow their operations. Americans will continue to come here to buy kids."

I saw the sincerity in his eyes. I thought of the Underground Railroad. What a risk they had taken! Defying insurmountable challenges, they had moved forward anyway. (At least what we were doing was completely legal, lawful, and under the jurisdiction of a legitimate government. The original Underground had to run outside of all that.) Guesno had the true spirit of Harriet Tubman—something I could only dream of attaining someday. I decided in that moment that we had no other choice. I told Guesno to green-light the operation.

"You won't be sorry," he reassured me with his bright smile. "And even if you become sorry, remember, we always have our contingency plan." I just shook my head at that. Yes, he did have a contingency plan. But it was so dangerous, I didn't even want to think about having to employ it.

◆　◆　◆

Super Bowl Sunday, February 5, 2017. The day of the operation had arrived. The Haitian police signed me up to play the role of the principal undercover American tourist. Because I had done quite a number of media appearances over the years, our volunteer Hollywood makeup artist fixed my face to the point that even my wife wouldn't recognize me.

Half a dozen traffickers ended up bringing more than two dozen victims to the beach party. The traffickers had been instructed by our undercover operators to deliver the children to a large cabana we had rented, which was part of the resort. They were then to make their way out to the yacht to negotiate the deal with me. Once the children arrived at the cabana, our undercover team of aftercare specialists (posing as the party planners, or "groomers") took over, received them, secured them, and began the process of rehabilitation. (This process is too sensitive to discuss in detail, but it only works in partnership with the top rehab programs within the country, including those run by private organizations.) The traffickers were to never have contact with their victims again.

As the children began their healing, the traffickers jumped into a small boat and rowed the short distance to visit me on the

The yacht used for the operation on Super Bowl Sunday

Tim Ballard negotiates with traffickers undercover

yacht. They wanted their payment. Apart from being the ideal prop to support our undercover identities, the yacht was also perfect for hiding cameras and recording devices. After welcoming the traffickers onto the boat, Cho among them, I sat them down and listened to them tell me about every child victim and what sexual acts they had performed and would perform. The undercover cameras aboard the yacht documented every word as a testimony against these wicked individuals—a testimony that will haunt them into eternity.

After I was done with them, I told them their money was waiting for them in a certain hotel room back at the resort. They rowed back to shore, went to the room, and received their pay from our undercover operators. When the deal was done, the call sign was given. The police rushed in and arrested Cho and all the other traffickers and took them to jail. Some of us were then whisked away to the airport and transported off the island. Guesno, Darius, and others of our brave operators and aftercare specialists stayed on the ground to see that the mission was completed.

I flew that night to Washington, D.C., as I had several appointments the next day with members of Congress regarding legislation we were working on. Many of them were aware of our operation and were anxious to hear the results, as our work affected their approach to creating new laws to combat human slavery around the world. I had gotten out of the country so fast that I was literally peeling back the prosthetic scars and wiping makeup off my face that very night in my D.C. hotel room. We all held our breath, praying that the Haitian judicial system would now kick in and do its job.

Several nights later, while I was still in D.C., my personal cell phone rang at 2 a.m., waking me up in my hotel room. I answered and heard death threats to me in a heavy Haitian Creole accent. To this day, I have no idea how they found my number or identified me. But instantly I knew: someone inside had betrayed us. It was only a matter of time before I learned that the majority of the traffickers had somehow been acquitted and released. Cho was back on the loose. Our nightmare had become reality.

I called Guesno upon receiving the news. "Guesno!" I yelled. "It happened! What are we going to do?!"

"I have activated the contingency plan, Tim," he told me. "I need you down in Haiti as soon as possible."

If my life was at risk, Guesno's situation was much worse because he lived on the small island and had nowhere to hide. But his love conquered his fear, and that love now sustained me.

The contingency plan was this: take the case to the media. Provide the evidence, which was as solid as any evidence I had ever collected in a case like this, and create a revolution against human trafficking in Haiti. This was extremely dangerous. We would be publicly outing powerful government officials and the traffickers they protected. They would hate us for that. And who knew to what extent they might go to silence us?

I had learned from Harriet Jacobs and Abraham Lincoln that when fighting the righteous cause of freedom, especially when taking risks to do so, miracles can be asked for and expected. We sought two specific miracles immediately. First, in the weeks after the Super Bowl operation, Haiti had elected a new president, Jovenel Moïse. Moïse had run on an anticorruption platform. If we could get his attention, perhaps he would help.

Second, we needed a voice the media and the people would listen to. Guesno told me he was arranging for the Rotary Club of Port-au-Prince to sponsor a media event, during which I could tell the story of what had happened. The Rotary Club was aware of a member of the U.S. Congress who was of Haitian descent. Her name was Mia Love. Her parents had immigrated to America from Haiti, and Mia became the first black female Republican ever to be elected to the U.S. Congress. That gave her celebrity status in Haiti.

"We need to get Mia Love, Tim," Guesno told me one night during a phone call. "The Rotary Club is certain that if we get Mia Love to the event, we can get the attention of the media and the new president. Do you know anyone who might know her?"

"Guesno!" I responded excitedly, "you won't believe this! For reasons completely unrelated to anything in Haiti, Mia happens to be one of my good friends."

When I called Congresswoman Love, I explained the risks of going into Haiti and publicly taking on traffickers and corrupt officials. But she didn't bat an eye at that. She only asked how soon we could go. In no time at all, the congresswoman and I were standing side by side in a Port-au-Prince conference room, telling the truth about human trafficking. The media was there, along with delegations sent by the president's office. Our message was clear: *Haiti is the original abolitionist nation.* We reminded them that in 1791, Haitian slaves did something that no other slave nation in history has ever done. Led by the slave-turned-warrior

Congresswoman Mia Love and Tim Ballard at the Haitian
Presidential Palace briefing President Jovenel Moïse about the
undercover operation and the corruption that followed

Toussaint Louverture, they began an unprecedented revolution: they rose up against their European masters, pushed them out, and took the island nation by force. The former slaves then became the national leaders. Under their new constitution, they abolished slavery and gave hope to a world still suffering under the plague of human bondage.

We quoted Frederick Douglass, who declared after the American Civil War: "We should not forget the freedom you and I enjoy . . . the freedom that has come to the colored race the world over, is largely due to the brave stand taken by the black sons of Haiti. . . . I regard her as the original pioneer emancipator of the nineteenth century."[94]

Our parting message to Haiti was a call to action, a plea: You inspired the world once before to end slavery, now please do it again!

Guesno's plan was working. The miracles continued dropping. After spending a few days reviewing our aftercare homes and pouring unconditional love into the children we had rescued (including little Mia and Marky), Congresswoman Love accompanied me to the Presidential Palace. We were going to meet with President Jovenel Moïse himself. In her perfect Haitian Creole, the congresswoman presented the evidence from the Super Bowl operation to the president and told him what had happened. She pled with him to fix the problem and help lead the world in the fight against human trafficking.

The president promised he would. And he was better than his word. He ordered an investigation and, within a few short months, the judges who had taken bribes from the traffickers we had arrested were found out and ripped from the bench.

The O.U.R. team was then invited to join and support Haitian officials in Operation Toussaint Louverture—the identification and re-arrest of Cho and the absolute dismantlement of her criminal organization. As O.U.R. possessed the majority of the intelligence regarding her whereabouts and her criminal patterns, we were thrilled to jump in. The office of the chief prosecutor, the body responsible for ending the reign of those corrupt judges, had been asked specifically by President Moïse to ensure this operation was successful. As it turned out, Cho had paid upwards of eighty thousand U.S. dollars to spring herself from jail the first time, and Haitian investigators had yet to determine who in the government had received the dirty money. So the president had more than one reason to bag Cho: rescue children and root out corruption.

Working with Haitian authorities, O.U.R. operators were able to identify the set of neighborhood blocks where Cho had set up operations in the wake of her arrest some ten months earlier. Whereas many of the lower traffickers from that initial arrest had gone into hiding and given up their criminal aspirations, Cho had had the audacity to pick up where she had left off.

I asked former Navy SEAL Dave Lopez (the same one about whom Coach Tomlin wrote in the Foreword) to work with Darius in putting together a tactically sound arrest plan to present to the Haitian authorities. Days before the operation was to take place, we gathered in a small hotel room in Port-au-Prince as Dave laid it all out. At the end of his first briefing, I asked him if he would pray for the success of the operation. After Dave had converted to God and light, he had become a devout Messianic Jew. When I asked him to pray, he knew exactly what I was asking for. It was prayer-song I had become accustomed to hearing Dave offer up before especially dangerous operations. The prayer, which he delivered in the Hebrew tongue, quoted special verses from Numbers 6:24–26: "The Lord bless thee, and keep thee: the Lord make his face shine upon thee, and be gracious unto thee: the Lord lift up his countenance upon thee, and give thee peace."

The only other prayer to rival this one in the days leading up to the operation was called for by Utah Attorney General Sean Reyes. A volunteer O.U.R. operator who assists on operations on his own time and with his own resources, Sean is a true friend to the cause. He had been a leader on the Super Bowl Sunday operation and was now back in Haiti with us to help finish the task. He had asked O.U.R. Director of Aftercare Jessica Mass to offer this prayer and invited Haitian officials and police officers to join hands with O.U.R. operators in a prayer circle. The prayer was a plea for the children—for the children we had already rescued, and especially for the ones still in captivity, the ones we now sought to liberate. There were few dry eyes in the room as Jessica said "Amen."

◆　◆　◆

"We have her in our sights. Positive ID." These were the adrenaline-inducing words I read on a text thread to me from our Recon-One unit. The Haitian police team, Haiti's chief prosecutor, and a handful of O.U.R. operators were crammed into a couple of hotel rooms a few blocks away from the commercial district where Recon-One had been surveying. We had chosen this hotel as our staging area based on intel we had gathered in the weeks prior—intel that put Cho's current criminal operation within the vicinity. The intel had proven correct. It could have been days before Cho surfaced, but fortunately she had reared her head within the first five hours after we had gathered at the hotel and deployed the recon teams. Recon-One provided the exact coordinates of Cho's current location. She was out on the street checking in on her dark enterprise.

I quickly moved from room to room sounding the quiet alarm for all units to mobilize and meet in the hotel basement parking lot, where our unmarked strike vehicles were waiting. Within moments we were throwing on our body armor and loading up into the vehicles. None of us knew how long we had before Cho disappeared again into her dark underworld. As we loaded the cars, Recon-One reported that Cho was still standing at the target location.

As the strike vehicles pulled out of the underground structure, I looked at my watch. We were only about three minutes from the target. Because we were uncertain of where Cho would ultimately emerge, and due to the secret nature of her "dens of nightmares," we never had any illusions that we would know ahead of time where the victims might be. But they would likely be close to where Cho was spotted. As we rolled out, we reminded our Haitian partners once again that as they exited the vehicles to make the arrest, they should simultaneously look for anything suspicious or unusual that may lead to further evidence, particularly as related to the whereabouts of Cho's victims. (It should be remembered that O.U.R. has no arrest authority but only works to coach and consult the police during their investigation.) The police wouldn't have warrants to search the doors that lined the streets. There would have to be a clear and legal reason for the police to breach any unknown building.

This is where we rely on our prayers. As we loaded into the cars, I sent out a prayer request to hundreds, if not thousands, of O.U.R. supporters: "WE NEED PRAYERS RIGHT NOW, THE KIND OF PRAYERS THAT CAN ONLY BE SAID ON YOUR KNEES. WE ARE ABOUT TO ROLL ON AN OPERATION IN A VERY DIFFICULT PART OF THE WORLD." I became emotional in the weeks that followed when I learned of moms and dads who immediately called their children together and knelt in prayer, and of business owners who dropped instantly to their knees with their employees in collective pleas to God. In that moment leading to action, our entire team felt the heavenly power emanating from such faithful supporters.

As we drove, I watched the face and hands of every passerby and simultaneously prayed: "Please let us find the kids! Please let us find the kids!" At T-minus two minutes, Jacob Justice, a videographer/evidence technician, interrupted my silent prayer when he leaped from the front of the van to the back where I was sitting. Stepping on my leg, he reached over to one of the three Haitian police officers sitting in the trunk seats. They had been assigned to pop the back hatch of the van when the team leader counted to three, and to immediately surround Cho, along with the other five police officers who were to exit through the front and side doors of our van.

"Jake, what are you doing?" I inquired anxiously.

"I don't know why, Tim," he explained, "but I have to get this GoPro camera onto the helmet of this cop."

I watched in amusement as Jake then placed the camera front and center on the cop's helmet, then began to rapidly wrap duct tape around and around the helmet until the camera was stable enough for Jake to release his grip on it. The sight and sound of the duct tape in action reminded me of a child clumsily wrapping a Christmas present for the first time. I laughed at the awkward scene. But the camera became secured as the tactical helmet morphed almost magically into what now looked like a miner's helmet.

"Youn, de, twa!" the team leader shouted as the van came to a screeching halt and doors from all sides of the van flew open. Boots hit the ground before the vehicles stopped, and in a matter of seconds Cho was surrounded, along with her three male minions. Handcuffs were placed on all four traffickers, and they were thrown into the back of a marked police truck that had

The police arrest Cho

been following our van close behind. It was over as fast as it had begun.

O.U.R. operators assisted the police in searching the street for evidence. (Among other things, we found Cho's assistant standing on a dark corner holding a large trash bag full of condoms. We counted over fifteen hundred condoms in the bag.) Within a few minutes of Cho being hauled off in the police truck, we looked up and saw a police officer walking slowly out of a red steel door directly across the narrow street from where Cho had just been arrested. Following closely behind him were three girls who looked to be about thirteen to fifteen years old. They wore thick makeup and were scantily clad. But the broken looks on their faces were what stood out the most.

The police officer also looked stunned. This is what had happened: As the police were exiting the strike vehicles to arrest Cho, one of them saw something out of the corner of his eye: a girl. Frightened by the scene, she ran a few yards from where she was standing on the street and entered through the red steel door to hide. The cop surreptitiously followed her and found himself standing inside one of Cho's dens of nightmares. At first he didn't know what to do—the scene was dark, wicked, and unexpected. There were victims there. There were rapists who had paid Cho to be there. And the cop had actually caught these rapists in the grotesque criminal act. All he could think to do in the moment was run through the dungeonlike room, pulling predators off of girls. He didn't feel he had time to call for backup. As he demanded that the predators put their clothes back on, he attended to the victims. And that was when the men dressed quickly and ran out the door, disappearing into the street.

We quickly went to the girls and got them into the safety of one of our vehicles. As we spoke to the police officer, he was still recovering from the scene and regretting that he had not grabbed the evildoers.

"They got away," the cop said regretfully.

"No, they didn't!" the voice of Jacob Justice piped up as he walked over to the police officer. Justice gripped the camera awkwardly protruding from the cop's helmet and ripped it from the mess of duct tape. We later confirmed that the camera had recorded it all! The men were identified and their criminal acts were caught on tape. Of the dozen or so cops on the arrest team that night, this was the *one* who had seen the girl run to the red door and enter it. This was the *one* who had then been led directly into the den of nightmares. It was a miracle.

Within a matter of hours, several additional arrests were made. In fact, as of the publication of this book, arrests and rescues continue to pour in as a result of this operation.

Hours after extracting the girls from the darkness, we placed them at one of our aftercare homes. O.U.R. Director of Aftercare, Jessica Mass, was there to escort them into the home. She knew what to do next. *Love* them. She provided them with all their basic needs, then began asking them what they wanted to be when they grow up. She encouraged them to dream big and assured them that she and the others at the home would be there to help them fulfill these dreams.

"We are your family," Jessica told them. "We are your family forever."

One of the girls finally spoke. With a small tear forming in her eye, she asked in a whispered voice, "Can I really hope now?"

Jessica smiled and nodded.

The girl continued: "I was only a small child when the earthquake hit. My parents were killed. That's when I was kidnapped, and I've been forced into this life ever since. That was exactly eight years ago. Eight years ago *today*."

Jessica looked at the calendar function on her phone. *Unbelievable.* The earthquake had struck on January 12, 2010. It was now January 12, 2018. The girl was right—*exactly* eight years to the day. The symbolism of the moment was not lost on anybody. It was nothing short of providential.

This girl's parents had named her Rosi. And she was beginning to understand that she was now free to become what her parents had always hoped she could become—the stars now being the only limits.

"I didn't realize until now that I was allowed to have dreams," she told Jessica, tears now flowing freely between both of them. "This is the first time in my life that I have experienced real hope."

Shortly after the operation, we discovered that the victims had a total of four babies, all born out of the difficult lives they were forced to live. Working with government officials and our partners on the ground, Jessica was able to secure all four babies and bring them to their very young mothers, into the safety of their new homes and new lives of restoration, love, and hope. The chain had been broken.

◆ ◆ ◆

When I look at the picture of Guesno in my office, I can't help but see the precious eyes of Rosi. I can't help but feel the light of hope. My mind flashes to the victims, to the children lost in the darkest corners of one of the most obscure nations on the planet. Who would have thought anyone would, or could, access them there? Certainly their traffickers felt safe to work their dark work. But no more! None of these captors are safe now. We will

*Tim Ballard confers with Guesno Mardy shortly after
the raid and rescue operation on Cho's brothel*

go to those dark corners the world over; we will go to those children who believe there is no hope left for them.

Because of Guesno, those children are now being liberated and restored one by one. And we will never stop until we find the last one. It's my promise to Guesno. It's *his* promise to his son. We *will* bring Gardy home.

On the night of Operation Toussaint Louverture, we all followed the police cars to the precinct and watched the jail doors close behind Cho and her evildoers. What then followed outside the jail were prayers of thanksgiving as Haitian police officers hugged O.U.R. operators. Attorney General Reyes pulled out several law-enforcement pins from his home office, and, to honor our partners, began pinning them on the collars of the Haitian heroes. There were cheers, slaps on the back, and more hugs.

Standing inside the happy chaos of celebration, I turned my head, and my eyes wandered, then fixed upon one man standing outside the group. He was standing alone, quietly taking it in, not wanting any recognition or even to be noticed. He had taken on the same quiet presence at the Super Bowl Sunday operation, at the media event with Mia Love, and at the planning and execution phases of this final operation. But he had been there for them all. He had been vital to them all. And though he wanted to remain hidden, the enormous smile on his face and the glow in his eyes betrayed his intent to go unseen. It silently flooded the scene and instantly became, at least to me, the most brilliant element around, as far as my eyes could see.

"The best way to find yourself is to lose yourself in the service of others."

—*Gandhi*

His name was Guesno Mardy.

CHAPTER 14

HARRIET JACOBS

I turned from the picture of Guesno, walked across my office floor, and stood in front of perhaps the most unassuming, and yet most powerful, piece of framed wall art in the room. It was a map of Harriet Jacobs's town: Edenton, North Carolina.

The map was an old one—older than Harriet herself. It showed the town as Harriet would have remembered it. I looked at King Street, focusing in on the exact property where stood Grandma Molly's home. The hiding place. The sacred spot of ultimate service and sacrifice. I glanced quickly at the Norcom property on Eden Street, smiled at the corner lot where Martha Blount lived, gave a nod to Snaky Swamp, and cringed at the site of the county jail. The map told the whole story of Harriet Jacobs. And of all the stories discussed in this book, none is quite as powerful to me as Harriet's, because her story reflects the truth of all the others. Her story, perhaps more than any other, teaches the lessons that were being revealed to me in the wake of my meeting with Burgess Owens. Especially the end of her story.

Harriet took her hard-won freedom and used it in the service of others. She sought every avenue she could to better the lives of others, especially her people who continued to toil under the demon slavery. One of Harriet's greatest accomplishments in fighting this evil was the writing and publication of her autobiography,

Historic map of Edenton, North Carolina

Incidents in the Life of a Slave Girl. Though she struggled to share intimate details of her sufferings in slavery, she knew that the world needed to understand how truly evil slavery was and how people, in both the North and the South, were responsible for allowing such evil to exist in their land. She hoped her book would help free more people.

"I feel that God has helped me," Harriet wrote, "or I never would consent to give my past life to any one for I would not do it without giving the whole truth. If it could help save another from my fate it would be selfish and unchristian in me to keep it back."[95]

Harriet's book was published in 1861, just as the Civil War was beginning. The timing could not have been better, for the war would become the tool that really began to wake the nation up to its crimes against humanity. Books like Jacobs's *Incidents in the Life of a Slave Girl,* Harriet Beecher Stowe's *Uncle Tom's Cabin* (also published shortly before the war), and other abolitionist materials would help soften hearts and bring people to seek a solution to the problem. Materials such as these opened the doors to the beginning of the end of nineteenth-century American slavery.

Jacobs's efforts in this cause have proven to be one of the most important lessons I have ever learned in combating modern slavery. As we have seen throughout this book, the most impressive servants in the cause of liberty—from Lincoln and Tubman to Guesno and little Mia—have always had one thing in common: they had *empathy.* When I fully allowed empathy to take over my heart while standing outside the gates of Mia and Marky's criminal orphanage, it changed every way I operated. These heroes of mine generally gained this empathy through their own suffering.

So how do we get others to a place of empathy, especially those who have never been exposed to the type of suffering that needs immediate attention? Like Harriet Jacobs did, we tell the true

THE END OF JAMES NORCOM

"Dr. Norcom is dead," Grandma Molly wrote to Harriet. "He has left a distressed family. Poor old man! I hope he made his peace with God" (*ILSG,* 252).

While Harriet was living, serving, and working in the North, her nemesis, James Norcom, continued his employment as a physician in the South. According to one account, while visiting a patient, Norcom fell down a flight of stairs, hitting his head. Doctors used the then-accepted medical technique of bleeding him in order to heal his wound. But they accidentally bled him to death.[96]

story boldly. This is why O.U.R. makes great efforts to film its operations and then show this footage to the public, to government administration officials, and to key members of the U.S. Congress, so that they know what's really going on and are able to *feel* it and then *act* on it. O.U.R. has used footage from its operations—in multiple briefings of congress and White House officials in furtherance of anti-trafficking legistlation, including H.R. 515: International Megan's Law, and other initiatives. We are forever grateful to Harriet and her colleagues in the cause for showing us how effective the tool of media can be against evil.

But writing and teaching against slavery was not enough for Harriet Jacobs. She wanted to get closer to the action. As the Civil War raged, she and Lulu moved into Southern territory, just behind the Union army lines. She did this so she could welcome runaway slaves fleeing to the North. With the Emancipation Proclamation in force, newly freed slaves were fleeing to the North by the thousands. Harriet provided

GRANDMA MOLLY'S FINAL WORDS

In one of her last letters to Harriet, Molly wrote:

"Dear Daughter,

I cannot hope to see you again on earth; but I pray to God to unite us above, where pain will no more rack this feeble body of mine; where sorrow and parting from my children will be no more. God has promised these things if we are faithful unto the end. . . . Thank your brother for his kindness. Give much love to him, and tell him to remember the Creator in the days of his youth, and strive to meet me in the Father's kingdom. . . . Strive, my child to train [Joseph and Lulu] for God's children. May he protect and provide for you, is the prayer of your loving old mother."

Molly died shortly after learning of and rejoicing in Harriet's full emancipation (*ILSG*, 251–52, 258).

many of them with food, clothing, shelter, and education. Ultimately, she established schools for her people. Harriet had provided a fine education for Lulu, who helped open and manage the Harriet Jacobs School (also known as the Jacobs Free School) in Alexandria, Virginia.[97] After the war, Harriet and Lulu would go deeper into the South to establish the Lincoln School for newly freed black children.

Harriet also sought out children who were orphaned by the war. She took them in and traveled with them to Northern states where she could more readily find families willing to adopt them.[98]

Once again, at Operation Underground Railroad, we have sought to apply these lessons to our modern-day mission. Like it was in Harriet's day, the rehabilitation and restoration phase of the rescue mission is of utmost importance. It is never a simple solution. As Harriet realized, such a restoration requires long-term care, perhaps even lifetime care. Though every case is different and requires a different approach, O.U.R. operators will not attempt a rescue operation unless and until qualified, long-term care is in place. We must assume in every case that the rescued child has no home or family to reunite with, because all too often that is the reality. We must be ready to provide this long-term care, which is why we support a wide range of after-care partners who provide basic needs, medical services, education, therapy (where necessary), and occupational training, so the survivor can learn to thrive and become whoever she or he wishes to become. We help provide these aftercare partners with what they need, and we regularly visit them, personally checking in on each survivor, to ensure everything that can be done is in fact being done.

We have also followed Harriet's example by working closely

THE SPIRIT OF THE CHILDREN

The Jacobs Free School in Alexandria, Virginia

"Slavery has not crushed out the animal spirits of these children. Fun lurks in the corners of their eyes, dimples their mouths, tingles at their fingers' ends, and is, like a torpedo, ready to explode at the slightest touch. . . . They never allow an older and stronger scholar to impose upon a younger and weaker one; and when they happen to have any little delicacies, they are ready to share them with others."[99]

—*Louisa "Lulu" Jacobs*

with adoption agencies, orphanages, and families wishing to adopt children. My wife, Katherine, recently cofounded the Children Need Families Foundation, which is dedicated to facilitating these adoption services.

Harriet also got more directly involved in the war effort. Through the Emancipation Proclamation, Lincoln opened the doors for black men to sign up as soldiers for the Union army. One of the first black infantries formed was the 54th Massachusetts. As they paraded one morning through the streets of Boston, Harriet was there to cheer them on. "How proud and happy I was that day," declared Harriet, "when I saw the 54th reviewed on Boston Common! How my heart swelled with the thought that my poor oppressed race were to strike a blow for freedom! Were at last allowed to help in breaking the chains."[100] The 54th fought so bravely and effectively that the nation was inspired to recruit more black soldiers. Lincoln credited these black recruits as tipping the scales of war in favor of the Union.

During a flag ceremony held to honor these black soldiers, Harriet Jacobs was asked to speak. "Soldiers," she declared, ". . . today you are in arms for the freedom of your race and the defense of your country—today this flag is significant to you.

One of the Union's black infantry regiments

Soldiers you have made it the symbol of freedom for the slave. . . . Then take the dear old flag and resolve that it shall be the beacon of liberty for the oppressed of all lands, and of every soldier on American soil."[101]

These lessons from Harriet Jacobs are timeless. Like hers were, even our most humble circumstances are often sufficient to educate the world about modern slavery and rehabilitate the survivors. She started as a slave, meaning almost no one had fewer resources to begin with than she did, yet she accomplished a great deal of good in the world by giving what she had in the spirit of empathetic service.

Flanking the map of Edenton on my office wall are depictions of Abraham Lincoln. That is fitting, for Harriet's story is incomplete without Lincoln's. Like Guesno, Harriet was not only focused on the individual rescue but also sought societal, systemic, and political change for her country. As president of the United States, Lincoln would take actions that would reflect the efforts Harriet and her fellow abolitionists were making to influence the nation.

It would take another hundred years in America to really see the fruits of Lincoln's message begin to emerge, and we still have not achieved the lasting peace he sought. Notwithstanding, in 1864, enough people got behind him to elect him to a second presidential term. Lincoln's main goal as he began his second term was to take the Emancipation Proclamation and make it permanent. Because it was a war measure, it was possible for the Emancipation Proclamation to be reversed once the war was over. Lincoln would make sure this did not happen by adding an amendment to the Constitution that outlawed slavery in every state forevermore. As Lincoln biographer Doris Goodwin pointed out, "Nothing on the home front . . . engaged

JOHN AND JONATHAN

John S. Jacobs, like his older sister, Harriet, knew the power of serving others, and so he dedicated his life to the abolitionist cause. Rather than focusing his new life of freedom on personal opportunity and wealth, John instead walked from town to town, teaching America of its sin of slavery and evangelizing the cause of human liberty. And he had a most interesting missionary companion in this effort. It was Captain Jonathan Walker, the original "Slave Stealer," the man who was arrested for assisting fugitive slaves in Florida and, as punishment, was branded with the letters *SS* on his hand.

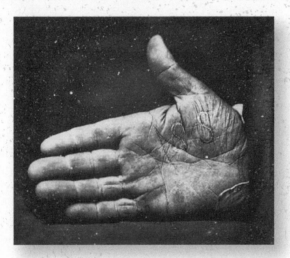

The *Herkimer Freeman* announced the duo's public appearance in New England: "That well-known sufferer for righteousness' sake, Capt. Jonathan Walker, an honest-hearted weather-beaten Christian sailor . . . arrived here on the 25th instant . . . and, after one more meeting here on New Year's night, expects to 'show his hand' among the people of the other sections of the country. He is accompanied from Boston by John S. Jacobs, 'a noble man of sable brow;' who, though but nine years since a Carolinian slave, has well improved his self-gained freedom, and speaks with fluency and depth of interest scarcely excelled by any of his predecessors—even Douglass himself."[103]

Lincoln with greater urgency than the passage of the Thirteenth Amendment."[102]

Harriet knew this was the only way to ensure freedom for her people, and she got behind Lincoln to fight for it. In 1863, the Women's National Loyal League was established in large part to push for this antislavery amendment. Harriet was asked to be on the executive committee of the League and offered the opening prayer at its meeting. In her prayer she asked the Almighty to "save the nation and free the slave."[104]

But Lincoln knew that the only path to ensure the Thirteenth Amendment would pass was to turn the people to heaven. If he could get them to desire a relationship with God, to repent, and to forgive and serve one another, then the people would naturally recognize the national sin of slavery and would vote to end it once and for all by supporting the new amendment. His Second Inaugural Address, given March 4, 1865, would teach these principles:

LINCOLN'S EFFORTS TO HEAL THE NATION

A few months after the Civil War battle of Gettysburg, Lincoln issued the Thanksgiving Proclamation, which established the national holiday on the last Thursday of every November and taught the formula for lasting peace and liberty. He explained that the great bounties in America were nothing but "the gracious gifts of the Most high God, who, while dealing with us in anger for our sins, hath nevertheless remembered mercy." He concluded this proclamation with a plea for the people to call upon God "with humble penitence for our national perverseness and disobedience" to heal "all those who have become widows, orphans, mourners or sufferers."[105]

Themes of turning to God and working to relieve the oppressed appeared throughout his writings and speeches until his death.

"Fondly do we hope, fervently do we pray, that this mighty scourge of war may speedily pass away. Yet, if God wills that it continue until all the wealth piled by the bondsman's two hundred and fifty years of unrequited toil shall be sunk, and until every drop of blood drawn by the lash shall be paid by another drawn by the sword, as was said three thousand years ago, so still it must be said 'the judgments of the Lord are true and righteous altogether.'" Lincoln then concluded: "With malice toward none, with charity for all, with firmness in the right as God gives us to see the right, let us strive on to finish the work we are in, to bind up the nation's wounds, to care for him who shall have borne the battle and for his widow and his orphan, to do all which may achieve and cherish a just and lasting peace among ourselves and with all nations."[106]

But was Lincoln's call to action going to have any effect? Would his plan to heal America through invoking the principles of love and service to God and man going to work? We have seen the formula bear fruit in individuals—indeed, it worked for Jacobs, Tubman, Mia, Guesno, and many others. But could it work for an entire nation? The evidence is encouraging.

In 2007, Harvard and Georgetown history professor Chandra Manning published the results of an extensive study she conducted regarding people's motives for fighting the Civil War. She collected notes, letters, camp newspapers, and publications from the North from the war years. Her conclusion: By the summer of 1863, more than six months after the Emancipation Proclamation, the general conclusion among the Union rank and file was that the "North had some real soul-searching to do before it could meet God's demands. Many soldiers felt sure that destroying slavery was necessary to gain God's favor, but . . . emancipation was not, by itself, enough to appease the Almighty."[107]

Manning continued: "By the Spring of 1865, the war had created a world almost no American could have recognized in 1861. White Union troops who might once have eschewed radical abolitionism now took pride in fighting to redeem the nation from the sin of slavery, and many took seriously the obligation to make ideals like freedom and equality into realities for black as well as white Americans."[108]

Like Harriet, Lincoln, Mia, and Guesno, the soldiers found themselves in a deep, dark hell. More people had died and were dying in the Civil War than have died in all other American wars combined up to and including World War II. (As Lincoln suggested in his Second Inaugural Address, this war represented "the judgments of the Lord" on the land.[109]) And like our other heroes, these soldiers apparently searched for a light to lead them out. The abolitionists and Lincoln were there to point them to that light: service to God and their fellow man, starting with the eradication of human bondage.

Harriet Jacobs had once asked, "Oh, when will the white man learn to know the hearts of my abused and suffering people."[110] It was at last beginning to happen.

Just weeks after Lincoln's Second Inaugural Address, the war finally ended. The Union had won a great victory over human bondage. In part to celebrate the victory, Lincoln took his wife to see a play at Ford's Theater. While there, he was shot and killed by a man who hated the ideals of freedom for all. But it was too late for the assassin. Too many people had already been converted to Lincoln's ideas. To show their love and support for their fallen president and his righteous vision, thousands of mourners stood along the train tracks that took his body back to his home in

SOLDIERS TESTIFY

"Any country that allows the curse of Slavery and Amalgamation as this has done should be cursed," according to one Illinois soldier, "and I believe in my soul that God allowed this war for the very purpose of cleaning out the evil and punishing us as a nation for allowing it."[113] Lt. Quincy Campbell agreed, claiming that "the chastisements of the Almighty are not yet ended . . . the Almighty has taken up the cause of the oppressed and . . . will deny us peace until we break every yoke and sweep every vestige of the cursed institution from our land."[114] Another soldier declared that until the nation repented of such crimes it could never "enjoy that peace which the nation has so long lost, and will never again have until made to know that God's image, of whatever hue, is worthy of respect, liberty and equality."[115]

In the election of 1864, Lincoln's opponent, George McClellan, promised to end the war if elected. Conversely, Lincoln vowed to continue to fight until slavery was dead. Eighty percent of the Union soldiers, even those who suffered the most, voted to retain their commander-in-chief, knowing that such a vote would keep them on the bloody battlefield until victory was achieved, which would mean they were quite possibly voting in their own death warrants.[116] Yet they knowingly did it.

Illinois. It was the largest funeral train ever recorded. Lulu was one of the thousands who went to his funeral and viewed his body. As she stood there, a tearful old woman turned to her and said, "They have killed our best friend. He was next to God. But child," the old woman noted, "they can't kill his work. They can't put the chains on us again."[111]

Lincoln's life work and vision culminated on December 6, 1865, some eight months after his death, when the Thirteenth Amendment became the law of the land. The nation had listened. The North could have defeated the South without then pushing for a Thirteenth Amendment. After all, that was the deal that had always been on the table for the South—an invitation to rejoin the Union and keep their precious slavery intact. But in the end, Lincoln had changed the offer and refused any Southern surrender that included the preservation of slavery.[112] Now the soldiers, and a growing number of the American populace, felt the same. They had felt the light of godly service. And they weren't about to let go now.

Though much work still needed to be done (and does even today), enough people chose the amendment, which means they chose to serve, to seek love, and to shine light in the darkness.

◆   ◆   ◆

The Thirteenth Amendment, while a major milestone, did not cure all our societal ills. The post–Civil War Reconstruction phase was generally dirty and divisive. Liberty, equality, and justice continue to be threatened today. The fight continues. Hate, prejudice, and divisiveness prevail and seem only to be growing today in America. What can we do? We can learn from history.

As Coach Tomlin pointed out in the Foreword to this book, we need to find unity, and what better way to unify than to come together around a cause that we can all support? We can all agree that the trafficking and enslavement of children is an abomination beyond description. So let's start there. Let's put down the weapons we hold against each other, call a truce, and gather around this societal plague, which represents one of the fastest-growing criminal enterprises on the planet. Let us all—of every color and creed—join hands and attack this wicked darkness together. Let's serve together. Let's serve one another.

Indeed, there is magic in service. If we have learned nothing else from the narratives in this book, it is that service, apart from the improvement it provides in the lives of those we reach, also touches our own lives. It enlightens us. It heals us—not only as individuals, but even as nations.

Let's not wait until darkness hits us (like it did the Union soldiers) before we start seeking the light. Let's serve each other now, find peace now, enjoy happiness now. If we do, perhaps the darker parts of history won't repeat themselves. Perhaps we will stave them off. Lincoln and the abolitionists created the medicine and began applying it to the wound—and it had great effect. But I fear we have forgotten. I fear we have stopped applying the medicine, and the national wound, rather than healing, is opening back up.

We have also learned that this formula (this "medicine") doesn't require us to serve just the cause of child trafficking (though that's a great place to start). It will work with any cause. Look around! Suffering and need are everywhere. If we spend more time seeking ways to love and serve each other, rather than seeking ways to hate and hurt each other, only then will the magic happen. Only then will the light kill the darkness. Only then will the healing begin. Only then will we at last be able to sit down and work out our many societal problems. There is a scientific law: light and dark cannot fill the same space at the same time. We have to choose one or the other. What will it be?

Let's turn to Harriet Jacobs to inspire us one last time to make the right choice.

Years after the war, Harriet, now in her seventies, was living in Washington, D.C., a successful businesswoman. Somebody brought the elderly Jacobs some interesting news. Though Dr. Norcom had died years earlier, what remained of the Norcom family had moved to Washington, D.C., and had fallen upon hard times. Dr. Norcom's grandchildren were going to bed hungry.

When Harriet learned of this, she certainly thought of how that family had treated her. She remembered the whippings and the beatings, and the constant threats that her children would be next. She remembered how Norcom had locked her children— two and six years old—in the county jail, and how he had tried to sell them to a place far away from their mother's loving arms. She remembered the years of painful separation from her children caused by Norcom's insatiable desire to own and abuse her. She remembered being denied marriage to the one man she loved. Yes, she remembered this family who with great effort had tried to destroy her life in every way possible.

And now she was just miles away from Norcom's suffering grandchildren—the very grandchildren Norcom had once threatened Harriet with, declaring out loud that Harriet "shall be my slave as long as I live, and when I am dead she shall be the slave of my children" (*ILSG*, 140). Yes, Harriet remembered all this. So, what would she do?

She gathered groceries. She prepared a great meal. She loaded up provisions. And she walked to 1011 11th Street North West, Washington, D.C.—the Norcom residence.[117]

Harriet Jacobs delivered love to the home of her enemy.

Harriet died in 1897 at the age of eighty-four. Her tombstone reads, "Patient in tribulation, fervent in spirit serving the Lord."

NOTES

General note: Throughout the book, notations *ILSG* refer to *Incidents in the Life of a Slave Girl: Written by Herself, with "A True Tale of Slavery," by John S. Jacobs,* by Harriet A. Jacobs, edited and with an introduction by Jean Fagan Yellin (Cambridge, MA: Belknap, 2009).

1. "Human trafficking: organized crime and the multibillion dollar sale of people," United Nations Office on Drugs and Crime, July 19, 2012, http://www.unodc.org/unodc/en/frontpage/2012/July/human -trafficking_-organized-crime-and-the-multibillion-dollar-sale-of-people .html.
2. Eric Foner, *Gateway to Freedom: The Hidden History of the Underground Railroad* (New York: W. W. Norton & Company, 2016), 15.
3. Some names, places, and incidental facts have been altered throughout this book in order to protect identities.
4. Some names and circumstances have been altered for security reasons.
5. "The Facts," Polaris, October 26, 2017, https://polarisproject.org /human-trafficking/facts.
6. http://www.ilo.org/global/about-the-ilo/newsroom/news/WCMS _243201/lang--en/index.htm; https://www.forbes.com/sites/kurtbaden hausen/2018/02/07/nba-team-values-2018-every-club-now-worth-at -least-1-billion/#2cac36007155; https://www.forbes.com/companies /starbucks/; https://www.forbes.com/companies/target/.
7. Rachel Swaner, Melissa Labriola, Michael Rempel, Allyson Walker, and Joseph Spadafore, "Youth Involvement in the Sex Trade: A National Study" (New York: Center for Court Innovation, 2016), https://www .ncjrs.gov/pdffiles1/ojjdp/grants/249952.pdf.
8. "The World Factbook: HAITI," Central Intelligence Agency, January 23, 2018, https://www.cia.gov/library/publications/the-world-factbook /geos/ha.html.
9. Trafficking in Persons Report 2017, U.S. Department of State, 194.

10. "Laws Passed by the General Assembly, 1823–31" (Raleigh, NC, 1832), 11.
11. Discovery made while the author searched and discussed the old membership records with Reverend Gilliam at the church, August 30, 2017.
12. Names and places have been changed for operational security.
13. Michael Tadman, *Speculators and Slaves: Masters, Traders, and Slaves in the Old South* (Madison: University of Wisconsin Press, 1996), 45.
14. Chowan County Deed Book L-2, 256.
15. Mary Ann Yannessa, *Levi Coffin, Quaker: Breaking the Bonds of Slavery in Ohio and Indiana* (Richmond: Friends United Press, 2001); Levi Coffin, *Reminiscences of Levi Coffin, the Reputed President of the Underground* (Cincinnati: Robert Clarke & Co., 1880).
16. Steve M. Miller and J. Timothy Allen, *Slave Escapes and the Underground Railroad in North Carolina* (Charleston, SC: History Press, 2016), 78.
17. Miller and Allen, *Slave Escapes,* 79–80.
18. https://www.wearethorn.org/child-pornography-and-abuse-statistics.
19. Coffin, *Reminiscences,* 12–13.
20. *The Edenton Woman's Club, A Walking Tour of Historic Edenton* (Edenton: Women's Club, 2015), 10, 66–67.
21. Harriet Jacobs to Amy Post, 1853, fragment in Isaac and Amy Post Family Papers; *ILSG,* 249, 255.
22. Jean Fagan Yellin, *Harriet Jacobs: A Life* (New York: Basic Civitas Books, 2004), 117.
23. "The Steamer 'Planter' and Her Captor," *Harper's Weekly,* June 14, 1862.
24. Henry Brown, *Narrative of the Life of Henry Box Brown* (Mineola, New York: Dover Publication, 2015), 41–53, originally printed in 1851.
25. William and Ellen Craft, *Running a Thousand Miles for Freedom* (Mineola, New York: Dover Publications, 2014), originally printed in 1860.
26. Solomon Northup, *Twelve Years a Slave: Narrative of Solomon Northup, a Citizen of New-York, Kidnapped in Washington City in 1841, and Rescued in 1853, from a Cotton Plantation near the Red River, in Louisiana,* edited by David Wilson (Auburn, NY: Miller, Orton & Mulligan, 1855).
27. Frederick Douglass to Harriet Tubman, in Sarah Hopkins Bradford, *Harriet, The Moses of Her People* (New York: Geo R. Lockwood & Son, 1897), 134–35.
28. Red Grigsby, as recorded in "Death of Sarah Lincoln," *Thomas Lincoln Family: Excerpts from Newspapers and Other Sources* (Lincoln Financial Foundation Collection), 11.
29. Joshua Wolf Shenk, *Lincoln's Melancholy: How Depression Challenged a President and Fueled His Greatness* (New York: Houghton Mifflin Company, 2005), 14.
30. Sarah Bush Lincoln interviewed by William Herndon, September 8,

1865, in *Herndon's Informants,* eds. Douglas L. Wilson and Rodney O. Davis (Illinois: University of Illinois Press, 1998), 109.

31. William H. Herndon and Jesse W. Weik, *Herndon's Lincoln,* 2 vols. (Springfield: The Herndon Lincoln Publishing Company, 1921), 1:75–76.

32. Mary Vineyard to William Herndon, July 22, 1866, in *Herndon's Informants,* 262.

33. Harriet Brent Jacobs to Amy Kirby Post, 185-, in Post Family Papers Project, https://rbsc.library.rochester.edu/items/show/459.

34. Cindy Weinstein, ed., *The Cambridge Companion to Harriet Beecher Stowe* (New York: Cambridge University Press, 2004), 1; Charles Edward Stowe, *Harriet Beecher Stowe: The Story of Her Life* (Boston: Houghton Mifflin Company, 1911), 203.

35. Joseph W. Holley, *You Can't Build a Chimney from the Top,* ed. Russell W. Ramsey (Lanham: University Press of America, 1948), 23.

36. David Goldfield, *America Aflame: How the Civil War Created a Nation* (New York: Bloomsbury Press, 2011), 75.

37. Roy Prentice Basler et al., eds., *The Collected Works of Abraham Lincoln,* 9 vols. (New Brunswick, NJ: Rutgers University Press, 1953), 4:250.

38. Abraham Lincoln, *Political Debates Between Abraham Lincoln and Stephen A. Douglas in the Celebrated Campaign of 1858 in Illinois: Including the Preceding Speeches of Each at Chicago, Springfield, Etc.* (OS Hubbell, 1895), 112.

39. Basler, *Collected Works of Abraham Lincoln,* 2:398–409.

40. Basler, *Collected Works of Abraham Lincoln,* 2:546.

41. Basler, *Collected Works of Abraham Lincoln,* 3:440.

42. Alexander H. Stephens, "Corner Stone Speech," Savannah, GA, March 21, 1861, http://teachingamericanhistory.org/library/document/cornerstone-speech/.

43. William C. Davis, *Jefferson Davis: The Man and His Hour* (New York: HarperCollins, 1991), 127, 177, 208, 212–13, 214, 216.

44. Stephens, "Corner Stone Speech."

45. Larry Schweikart and Michael Patrick Allen, *A Patriot's History of the United States: From Columbus's Great Discovery to the War on Terror* (New York: Penguin, 2004), 298.

46. "Declaration of the Immediate Causes Which Induce and Justify the Secession of South Carolina from the Federal Union and the Ordinance of Secession" (Charleston, SC: Evans and Cogswell, Printers to the Convention, 1860), 7.

47. Stephens, "Corner Stone Speech."

48. William J. Davis, *Jefferson Davis: The Man and His Hour* (New York: HarperCollins, 1991), 495.

49. Chandra Manning, *What This Cruel War Was Over: Soldiers, Slavery, and the Civil War* (New York: Alfred A. Knopf, 2007), 32. The scope of this study does not permit an exhaustive list of the many publications, sermons, and other communications in the South, which clearly prove that the Southern war cause was sustained by a passion to preserve the practice of slavery. For more on this, see David Goldfield, *America Aflame: How the Civil War Created a Nation* (New York: Bloomsbury Press, 2011), 183–96.

50. Herndon and Weik, *Herndon's Lincoln,* 1:75–76.

51. Frederick Douglass, *Life and Times of Frederick Douglass Written by Himself* (Boston, MA: De Wolfe, Fiske, and Co., 1895), 430–31.

52. Elizabeth Keckley, *Behind the Scenes, or, Thirty Years a Slave, and Four Years in the White House* (New York: G.W. Carleton & Co., 1868), 103.

53. Keckley, *Behind the Scenes,* 104.

54. Keckley, *Behind the Scenes,* 103.

55. David Von Drehle, *Rise to Greatness: Abraham Lincoln and America's Most Perilous Year* (New York: Henry Holt and Company, 2012), 77.

56. F. B. Carpenter, *The Inner Life of Abraham Lincoln: Six Months at the White House* (Lincoln, NB: University of Nebraska Press, 1995; originally published New York, 1886), 30–31.

57. Richard J. Carwardine, *Lincoln: Profiles in Power* (Harlow: Pearson, 2003), 221.

58. Carwardine, *Lincoln,* 221.

59. Noah Brooks, "Recollections of Lincoln," *Harper's Magazine* 31, no. 210 (June 1865): 226, https://books.google.com/books?id=AAUw AAAAMAAJ&pg=PA226.

60. John D. Defrees to William H Herndon, in *Herndon's Informants,* eds. Douglas L. Wilson and Rodney O. Davis (Urbana and Chicago, IL: University of Illinois Press, 1998), 497.

61. Carwardine, *Lincoln,* 221.

62. Harriet Jacobs to [J] Sella Martin, Alexandria, April 13 [1863], "Letter from Mrs. Jacobs," in Harriet A. Jacobs, John S. Jacobs, Louisa Matilda Jacobs, and Jean Fagan Yellin, *The Harriet Jacobs Family Papers* (Chapel Hill: University of North Carolina Press, 2008), 477–88.

63. Basler, *Collected Works of Abraham Lincoln,* 6:535–36.

64. Basler, *Collected Works of Abraham Lincoln,* 5:279; 5:478.

65. Carwardine, *Lincoln,* 225.

66. Carwardine, *Lincoln,* 209.

67. Carwardine, *Lincoln,* 231.

68. Carwardine, *Lincoln,* 221.

69. Frederick Douglass, in James McPherson, *The Negro's Civil War: How*

American Blacks Felt and Acted During the War for the Union (New York: Vintage Books, 2003), 17.

70. Harriet Jacobs to Amy Post, Idlewild, December 8 [1862] #50. Isaac and Amy Post Family Papers.

71. John S. Jacobs to Isaac Post, "A Colored American in England," in Jacobs et al., *Harriet Jacobs Family Papers*, 353–54.

72. Harriet Beecher Stowe, *Uncle Tom's Cabin* (New York: A. L. Burt, 1852), 484.

73. Gideon Welles, *Diary of Gideon Welles: Secretary of the Navy under Lincoln and Johnson* (Boston, MA: Houghton Mifflin, 1911), 1:70.

74. John Niven, ed., *The Salmon P. Chase Papers, Volume 1: Journals, 1829–1872* (Ohio: The Kent State University Press, 1993), 343.

75. Basler, *Collected Works of Abraham Lincoln,* 5:278–79, 403–4; emphasis added.

76. John M. Hay and John G. Nicolay, *Abraham Lincoln: A History,* 10 vols. (New York: Cosimo Classics, 2009), 6:342.

77. Welles, *Diary of Gideon Welles,* 1:143.

78. James M. McPherson, "If The Lost Order Hadn't Been Lost," in Robert Cowley, ed., *What If? The World's Foremost Military Historians Imagine What Might Have Been* (New York: Penguin Putnam Inc, 1999), 231–32.

79. Frederick Douglass, "Oration in Memory of Abraham Lincoln," in *Frederick Douglass: Selected Speeches and Writings* (1876): 615–24.

80. See McPherson, "If The Lost Order Hadn't Been Lost," 231–32.

81. McPherson, "If The Lost Order Hadn't Been Lost," 232.

82. Carwardine, *Lincoln,* 210, 228.

83. Von Drehle, *Rise to Greatness,* 369.

84. Carwardine, *Lincoln,* 210, 228.

85. Gideon Welles, *Diary of Gideon Welles,* 1:143.

86. Schweikart and Allen, *Patriot's History,* 343.

87. *National Anti-Slavery Standard,* June 6, 1863, 3.

88. Kevin Bales, *Ending Slavery* (Berkley: University of California Press, 2007), 2.

89. Carwardine, 180, 203.

90. James M. McPherson, *Abraham Lincoln and the Second American Revolution* (New York: Oxford University Press, 2007), 34.

91. Basler, *Collected Works of Abraham Lincoln,* 6:28–30.

92. Carwardine, 193.

93. Martin Luther King, Jr., "The Drum Major Instinct" (1968), in Clayborne Carson and Peter Holloran, *A Knock at Midnight: Inspiration from the Great Sermons of Reverend Martin Luther King, Jr.* (Grand Central Publishing, 2001).

94. Frederick Douglass, "Lecture on Haiti," in *The Haitian Revolution:*

A Documentary History, ed. David Geggus (Indianapolis: Hackett Publishing Company, Inc., 2014), 204–5.

95. Jacobs to Post, [1852?], Isaac and Amy Post Family Papers #84, Black Abolitionist Papers 16:0700–02 (Letter 4).

96. "Dr. James Norcom," Findagrave.com, https://www.findagrave.com /memorial/25175277#.

97. *ILSG,* vi; Yellin, *Harriet Jacobs: A Life,* 178, 259.

98. See Yellin, *Harriet Jacobs: A Life,* 168–69, 199.

99. Harriet Jacobs and Louisa M. Jacobs to L. Maria Child, March 26, 1864, in *National Anti-Slavery Standard,* April 16, 1864.

100. Harriet Jacobs to L. Maria Child, quoted in L. Maria Child to Francis George Shaw, October 18, 1863, Houghton Library, Harvard University, Child Papers.

101. *"Physicians, Soldiers, and Friends"* "Flag Presentation at L'Ouverture Hospital, Alexandria, Va.," *Anglo-African,* September 3, 1864.

102. Doris Kearns Goodwin, *Team of Rivals: The Political Genius of Abraham Lincoln* (New York: Simon & Schuster, 2006), 686.

103. "The Walker Meetings," *National Anti-Slavery Standard,* January 6, 1848, taken from the *Herkimer Free-man.*

104. "Women's Loyal National League," *New York Tribune,* October 30, 1863.

105. Basler, *Collected Works of Abraham Lincoln,* 6:496–97.

106. Basler, *Collected Works of Abraham Lincoln,* 8:332–33.

107. Manning, *What This Cruel War Was Over,* 118–19.

108. Manning, *What This Cruel War Was Over,* 211.

109. Abraham Lincoln, Second Inaugural Address, March 4, 1865, https:// cdn.loc.gov/service/mss/mal/436/4361300/4361300.pdf.

110. Harriet Jacobs to L. Maria Child, March 1863; in *National Anti-Slavery Standard,* April 18, 1863.

111. Louisa Jacobs, Alexandria, April 27, 1865, "Fourth Report of a Committee of Representatives of New York Yearly Meeting of Friends upon the Condition and Wants of the colored Refugees," 10.

112. Goodwin, *Team of Rivals,* 647.

113. Capt. Amos Hostetter, Thirty-fourth III, to sister and brother-in-law, January 29, 1863, Murfreesboro, Tennessee (Springfield: Illinois State Historical Library).

114. Mark Grimsley, *Union Must Stand: The Civil War Diary of John Quincy Adams Campbell* (Knoxville: The University of Tennessee Press, 2016), 110.

115. Manning, *What This Cruel War Was Over,* 165.

116. Manning, *What This Cruel War Was Over,* 185.

117. Julia Wilbur Diary, June 4, 1885.

INDEX

Page numbers in *italics* refer to images.

PHOTO CREDITS

Page viii: Photo by Jacob Justice, courtesy Operation Underground Railroad (O.U.R.)

Page 9: Shutterstock.com/Everett Historical

Page 17: Shutterstock.com/Jeffrey M. Frank

Page 19: Photo by Anne Ballard

Page 33: Photo by Ramy Romany and Nick Nanton, courtesy O.U.R.

Page 48: Photo by Tim Ballard

Page 53: Photo by Mike Porenta, courtesy O.U.R.

Page 55: Photo by Guesno Mardy

Page 61: Images by Hillary Newton, courtesy O.U.R.

Page 67: Photo by Anne Ballard

Page 71: Photo by Anne Ballard

Page 83: Photo by Jake Christensen

Page 85: Photo by Anne Ballard

Page 89: Shutterstock.com/Sarah Nicholl

Page 108: Photo by Mark Mabry, courtesy O.U.R.

Page 115: Photo by Mark Mabry, courtesy O.U.R.

Page 118: Photo by Carol M. Highsmith, courtesy Library of Congress

Page 137: Shutterstock.com/Rakdee

Page 166: Photo by Benjamin F. Powelson, courtesy Library of Congress

Page 171: Photo by George Francis Schreiber, courtesy Library of Congress

Page 174: Photo by S. M. Fassett, courtesy Library of Congress

Page 183: Shutterstock.com/Sergey Shubin

Page 183: Library of Congress

Page 195: Shutterstock.com/Everett Historical

Page 207: Photo by Mark Mabry, courtesy O.U.R.

Page 209: Photo by Jake Christensen, courtesy O.U.R.

Page 210: Photo by Jake Christensen, courtesy O.U.R.

Page 213: Photo by Jacob Justice, courtesy O.U.R.

Page 218: Photo by Ramy Romany and Nick Nanton, courtesy O.U.R.
Page 222: Photo by Ramy Romany and Nick Nanton, courtesy O.U.R.
Page 230: Shutterstock.com/Everett Historical
Page 236: Library of Congress

All other photos in public domain